No High Lik

THE
MOST
HIGH

Divine Direction for Destiny

By
Kent Mattox

McDougal Publishing is a ministry of The McDougal Foundation, Inc., a Maryland nonprofit corporation dedicated to spreading the Gospel of the Lord Jesus Christ to as many people as possible in the shortest time possible.

Published by:

McDougal Publishing
P.O. Box 3595
Hagerstown, MD 21742-3595
www.mcdougal.org

ISBN 1-884369-90-1

Printed in the United States of America
For Worldwide Distribution

Not as though I had already attained, either were already perfect: but I follow after, if that I may apprehend that for which also I am apprehended of Christ Jesus. Brethren, I count not myself to have apprehended: but this one thing I do, forgetting those things which are behind, and reaching forth unto those things which are before, I press toward the mark for the prize of THE HIGH CALLING OF GOD in Christ Jesus. Philippians 3:12-14

ACKNOWLEDGMENTS

I would like to say a special thanks:

To my wife, Beverly, for tirelessly editing this manuscript. She not only is a great editor, mother and wife, she is also my best friend, with whom I pray to grow old and wrinkled.

To my daughter-in-law, Lori, for diligently inputting this manuscript and for continually putting up with my idiosyncrasies and detailed ways.

To my two sons, Joshua and Caleb. To Joshua, whom God has called as my ministry associate and who amazes me with his wisdom and understanding. To Caleb, who brings us all joy and has taught me so much about God. I pray they always walk in the High Places.

To Pastor Benny, for without his obedience to the Holy Spirit, I would not be in the ministry today.

Most of all, to my Friend in High Places, Jesus. There is none like You in all the universe.

CONTENTS

FOREWORD BY BENNY HINN

Kent Mattox worked with me for many years and is a very precious man, as well as a powerful instrument of God. He was used to be a great blessing and strength to my life. I love him and Beverly.

We've had great experiences together, Kent and I. He traveled with me for a long time. I'll never forget the many times we prayed together. He became my prayer partner, and it seems that everything Kent and I would agree on together in prayer the Lord would answer.

There was a supernatural impartation of understanding given to Kent by the Holy Spirit to serve and protect the anointing on my life and ministry. This does not come by learning, but only by the touch of God upon one's life.

I knew this man when he started, and to see what God has done in him and through him is a great miracle. A great wealth has been deposited in him by the Lord.

As I have sown Kent (if I may say so) into the nations, in being a part of fulfilling God's destiny for his life, I pray that a bountiful harvest of the wealth that is in him is reaped by those to whom he ministers. As you read *No High Like THE MOST HIGH*, it is my heartfelt desire that, through Kent's personal experience and teachings, you truly are blessed and that God's divine destiny will be fulfilled in your own life.

INTRODUCTION

For just a moment, let your imagination run free. Imagine the exhilaration of a mountain climber scaling the heights and finally reaching the top, planting his banner on the highest peak. Consider the thrill of being at bat with the bases loaded, two outs, two strikes, and your crushing grand slam wins the game. Think of the excitement of standing at the altar anticipating the arrival of your bride as she is escorted down the aisle. The beautiful processional music swells around you both, and tears of joy fall as the two become one.

In life, many highs mark the passage of time and highlight our development and growth. As we make life's journey, there are exciting new beginnings along the way — seeing our first child come into the world, entering into our first career or feeling the pride of achievement when our hard work pays off and we receive our first raise or promotion. With each new opportunity in life there is a sense of fulfillment and satisfaction, a tangible sense of accomplishment.

Whether we are blessed to experience the thrill of victory in family, career or sports, there are moments in our lives that stand out above the everyday experiences. From the moment we draw our first breath to begin life until we breathe our last, there will always be high moments that are set apart in our memories as being special, as being great, and it's from these times that we often draw when we need a lift from the everyday task of living.

No matter how fulfilled you have been, no matter how successful you have become, no matter how high your highs have been, there is a place that is higher — higher than your fulfillment, higher than your successes, higher than your highest high. That place is found in the Lord Jesus Christ. We have been supernaturally custom-designed to desire a relationship with Him. In every individual there is a space just waiting to be filled with the indwelling presence of His Holy Spirit.

As you read *No High Like THE MOST HIGH* I pray that the revelation of God's presence manifests itself in your life like never before. Get ready as your journey to the High Places continues.

God wants you to have the strength to overcome any obstacle preventing you from reaching the High Places in Him. No matter how high you have already gone or how low you have fallen, He has a plan for you that is greater than anything you could have ever imagined.

CHAPTER 1

SEEKING THE HIGHEST HIGH

He maketh my feet like hinds' feet, and setteth me upon my high places.
Psalm 18:33

After our greatest successes in life, we each come to realize that there is still an existing emptiness in us, one that nothing seems to fill. No matter how long we have searched for fulfillment or how hard we have worked to achieve it, there is still something missing in our lives. That empty space was created for one purpose, and it can only be filled by the One who created it. The only way to have complete peace and fullness of joy in life is through an intimate relationship with the Creator — the Most High God! The Bible declares:

He made him ride on the high places of the earth, that he might eat the increase of the fields; and he made him to suck honey out of the rock, and oil out of the flinty rock. Deuteronomy 32:13

God wants to take you higher than you have ever been before. All the pinnacles and summits of this world are counterfeits compared with the real High Places that He wants to share with you.

The book of Deuteronomy tells us of God's plan to show us the High Places He has prepared for us:

And it shall come to pass, if thou shalt hearken diligently unto the voice of the LORD *thy God, to observe and to do all his commandments which I command thee this day, that the* LORD *thy God will set thee on high above all nations of the earth.*   Deuteronomy 28:1

God's plans for you are greater than any you could ever create for yourself. His desire is to *"set [you] on high above all nations of the earth"* (see also Revelation 2:26). Most of us would never aspire to such a lofty goal on our own!

Once God is working in your life, filling that empty place that He designed especially for Himself, He begins to fulfill His promises to you.

There is nothing more comforting than to know that God is with us. The psalmist assures us of safety in God's presence:

He that dwelleth in the secret place of the most High shall abide under the shadow of the Almighty. I will say of the LORD, *He is my refuge and my fortress: my God; in Him will I trust. Surely he shall deliver thee from the snare of the fowler, and from the noisome pestilence. He shall cover thee with his feathers, and under his wings shalt thou trust: his truth shall be thy shield and buckler. Thou shalt not be afraid for the terror by night; nor for the arrow that flieth by day; nor for the pestilence that walketh in darkness; nor for the destruction that wasteth at noonday. A thousand shall fall at thy side, and ten thousand at thy right hand; but it shall not come nigh thee. Only with thine eyes shalt thou behold and see the reward of the wicked.*

Because thou hast made the LORD, *which is my refuge, even the most High, thy habitation; there shall no evil befall thee, neither shall any plague come nigh thy dwelling. For he shall give his angels charge over thee, to keep thee in all thy ways. They shall bear thee up in their hands, lest thou dash thy foot against a stone. Thou shalt tread upon the lion and adder: the young lion and the dragon shalt thou trample under feet. Because he hath set his love upon me, therefore will I deliver him: I will set him on high, because he hath known my name. He shall call upon me, and I will answer him: I will be with him in trouble; I will deliver him, and honour him. With long life will I satisfy him, and shew him my salvation.*   Psalm 91

God's highs are greater than anything you could ever imagine! His Word declares:

Eye hath not seen, nor ear heard, neither have entered into the heart of man, the things which God hath prepared for them that love him.
                                                                    1 Corinthians 2:9

God has a great destiny for you, planned from the foundations of the Earth, and His desire for His children is for them to dwell in His High Places. Most of us have only begun to climb.

As we go the distance, climbing to ever higher heights, it is through the times we stumble and fall that we see God's hand most clearly. He is constantly encouraging and strengthening us to forge ahead and conquer whatever stands in the way of victory. During these times, *"[His] Word is a lamp unto [our] feet, and a light unto [our] path"* (Psalm 119:105).

Our human limitations prevent us from comprehending the mountaintop experiences that God ultimately has for us. No earthly pleasure can compare with the splendor of the High Places of God.

When we sense God's presence most, it is in the furnace of affliction, not high on the mountaintop. Most likely that is why there is far more time spent dealing with the trials of life than with the triumphs. If we spent all our time going from victory to victory, there would be no reason to seek God's will. It is during the times we experience personal pain, sorrow and suffering that we turn to Him as Comforter, as the Most High God, who will never forsake us. During these times we come to know Him intimately and are drawn to His comfort.

As the Most High reveals more of His plan for us and takes us higher in Him, the things of this world grow smaller and smaller, because He is lifting us higher and higher. This is how He wants us to live our lives, staying focused on where He is taking us, not on where we have been. Paul made this perfectly clear in his letter to the Ephesians:

> *Even when we were dead in our transgressions, [God, the Most High] made us alive together with Christ, [He saved us by His grace and mercy] and raised us up with Him ... in the heavenly places, in Christ Jesus.* Ephesians 2:5-6, NNAS

As you begin your journey into the High Places of God, let Him transform you from being earthly-minded to being heavenly-minded. Let Him give you the ability to overcome whatever circumstances, issues or problems are holding you back from the mountaintop. He wants to give you hinds' feet, just as He did to David when his enemies were pursuing him. David was able to sing:

> *He maketh my feet like hinds' feet, and setteth me upon my HIGH PLACES.* Psalm 18:33

Although this was the confession David made by faith, the reality of his life at that moment was quite different. He was actually hiding in a cave waiting for his day of deliverance. By faith, however, he received *"hinds' feet."*

God wants you to become as sure-footed as a hind (a deer or hart) so you can walk in the High Places with Him. If you have ever seen a deer leaping majestically from place to place, you realize the power these animals have to escape from danger. While being pursued, they accomplish the amazing and incredible feat of leaping across dangerous terrain and over tall barriers to overcome anything in their way and make it to safety. God wants you to have the strength to overcome any obstacle preventing you from reaching the High Places in Him.

Regardless of how high you have already gone or how low you have fallen, God has a plan for you that is greater than anything you could have ever imagined. While we are in the midst of overcoming life's difficulties, He has made us a promise on which we can stand, that one day we will rule and reign with Him:

> *After these things I looked, and behold, a door standing open in heaven, and the first voice I heard, like the sound of a trumpet speaking with me, said, "Come up here, and I will show you what must take place after these things." Immediately I was in the Spirit; and behold, a throne was standing in heaven, and One sitting on the throne.*
>
> Revelation 4:1-2, NNAS

GET READY! God is taking us to the High Places. As we go higher and higher, the problems of this world will seem as though they had never existed. Our God is with us. He has promised never to leave us nor forsake us. He is the glory and the lifter of our heads. He is THE MOST HIGH God!

It is God who works His will in you. Not only is He working out the details of your life to fulfill your destiny, He will also give you the will to fulfill it.

CHAPTER 2

FULFILLING YOUR DIVINE DESTINY

If I ascend up into heaven, thou art there: if I make my bed in hell,
behold, thou art there. Psalm 139:8

You are never too high, never too low, never too far from God!
The Word of God declares:

Blessed be the God and Father of our Lord Jesus Christ, who hath blessed
us with all spiritual blessings in heavenly places in Christ: according as
he hath chosen us in him before the foundation of the world, that we
should be holy and without blame before him in love.
Ephesians 1:3-4

Before the foundation of the world was even laid, God was
planning your destiny. Think about that. The Apostle Paul went
on to say:

In whom also we have obtained an inheritance, being predestinated
according to the purpose of him who worketh all things after the coun-
sel of his own will. Verse 11

Can you grasp the magnitude of this truth? You have a divine
destiny, a plan that God made just for you. That plan may not be

what you are now walking in, and you may not have even realized that there is a divine destiny for your life, but if you will give God the liberty to manifest Himself in you and to you, He will bring your destiny to light.

David's psalm to his chief musician declares that God's Spirit is always with us:

O LORD, thou hast searched me, and known me. Thou knowest my downsitting and mine uprising; thou understandest my thought afar off. Thou compassest my path and my lying down, and art acquainted with all my ways. For there is not a word in my tongue, but, lo, O LORD, thou knowest it altogether. Thou hast beset me behind and before, and laid thine hand upon me. Such knowledge is too wonderful for me; it is high, I cannot attain unto it.

Whither shall I go from thy spirit? or whither shall I flee from thy presence? If I ascend up into heaven, thou art there: if I make my bed in hell, behold, thou art there. If I take the wings of the morning, and dwell in the uttermost parts of the sea; even there shall thy hand lead me, and thy right hand shall hold me.

… Surely the darkness shall cover me; even the night shall be light about me.

For thou hast possessed my reins: thou hast covered me in my mother's womb.

Thine eyes did see my substance, yet being unperfect; and in thy book all my members were written, which in continuance were fashioned, when as yet there was none of them.   Psalm 139:1-11, 13 and 16

It doesn't matter how high your successes have taken you or how low your failures have caused you to plummet. God is there. When you were yet in your mother's womb, God already knew you. He is working His will in you, regardless of the circumstances of your life:

For it is God which worketh in you both to will and to do of His good pleasure. Philippians 2:13

It is God who works His will in you. Not only is He working out the details of your life to fulfill your destiny, but He also gives you the will to fulfill it. You may have gotten off course and ended up in a backslidden state, you may never have served God in any way, or you may be searching for the will of God as a believer. If any of these statements describes the situation you are in, don't despair. You can never go so far that God cannot hear your cries. Just lift your voice to Him. The Apostle Paul declared:

For I am persuaded, that neither death, nor life, nor angels, nor principalities, nor powers, nor things present, nor things to come, nor height, nor depth, nor any other creature, shall be able to separate us from the love of God, which is in Christ Jesus our Lord. Romans 8:38-39

We cannot even begin to comprehend the unconditional love of God. In his letter to the Ephesians, Paul showed us how to grasp the depth of that love:

That Christ may dwell in your hearts by faith; that ye, being rooted and grounded in love, may be able to comprehend with all saints what is the breadth, and length, and depth, and height; and to know the love of Christ, which passeth knowledge, that ye might be filled with all the fulness of God. Ephesians 3:17-19

Christ Jesus HAS ALREADY paid the price on Calvary's cross! No matter how high success has taken you, His love is there. No matter how deeply entrenched in sin your life may have become, His love is there. No matter how far away from God you may feel, His love is there. His love will draw you to Him so that His plan for your life will ultimately be fulfilled.

I can take you to the very place where, as a teenage boy, I made the decision to leave my destiny in God and seek the pleasures of the world. Since I was raised in a Christian home, I had experienced the presence of God in my life. Now the world and all its hidden secrets were luring me, calling me to come and taste the forbidden things that my imagination teased me with. Sin and all its counterfeit promises were a mighty lure, pulling me away from what I had been raised to believe. It was, in the end, a force too strong for me to resist.

My folks, Tom and Peggy Mattox, always made sure that their children attended church on Sunday. Although I was the youngest of five, I was no exception, and every Sunday morning found me sitting in the congregation in which I was raised.

I tried to live the Christian life. I must have gotten saved fifty times by the time I made that fateful decision to turn my back on God. Every Sunday the conviction of the Holy Spirit would touch me, and I would make my way to the altar and pour my heart out to God, asking Him to forgive me of my sins. Each time I would receive forgiveness, but then on Monday I would go right back into the world. Does that sound familiar? Although I had been raised in church, I had not really been taught about the power of the Word of God. I did not know, for instance, that through His Word God had given me weapons of warfare I could use to fight the battle that was raging between my soul and my spirit (see Ephesians 6:11-18).

My fateful decision took place in our home. One morning when I was seventeen years old, while standing in the shower, I said to the Lord: "If You will just let me have the next two or three years to enjoy the things of the world, then I will serve You." I wish I had known at that moment what the decision I had just made would cost me. God never enters into agreements that glorify the flesh! He is a jealous God, and He guards His love jealously!

The most amazing facet of God's love is how longsuffering and steadfast it is. I turned my back on Him and His plan and began a journey of seeking the things I thought would take me higher. Little did I know that the hunger I had for financial success and recognition would ultimately send me into a downward spiral that would take me to the lowest point in my life.

Not surprisingly, after I made this decision I no longer felt conviction when I attended church. It was not very long after the proclamation in the shower that I stopped attending church altogether.

My parents were affiliated with a large corporation that allowed them, as independent contractors, to work as little or as much as they chose. What they earned was up to them. As soon as I graduated from high school, I joined forces with them and began accumulating a little nest egg for myself. I seemed to have a natural affinity for sales, and I did well.

Just as soon as I had accumulated enough cash to finance an investment of my own, I went into business with a friend of mine. We opened an arcade where young people could play games and dance. Since we did not sell alcoholic beverages there, the place was a big hit with both the parents and the kids. The arcade was packed, and we were making money hand over fist.

We decided to invest in yet another venture, however our choice this time did not prove to be a good one. We ended up losing what we had put into the business and then some.

I was only nineteen years old, but I had developed a taste for the finer things in life, and I needed money to sustain my lifestyle. After the collapse of this latest financial venture, I decided to try my hand in the real estate market. Vacation packages had become very popular in America in the early eighties, and I thought I might do well selling them.

My pursuit of new financial highs took me to Myrtle Beach,

South Carolina, and there I made money more quickly than I had ever thought possible. I seemed to have a natural aptitude for selling real estate, and my skills in sales were becoming more fine-tuned all the time.

As money poured into my bank account, I felt successful, recognized and prosperous. With all of my immediate needs met — a place to live, transportation, food and friends — there was plenty of money left over to spend on pursuing the accoutrements I had come to believe went with the level of success I had quickly attained. As part of a large, loving family, I knew that ultimately I desired to have a wife and a family, but for the time being, such thoughts were put away on a shelf.

After a while I sensed that the life I had created for myself was pulling me further and further into a deep hole. In moments of despair, I would pull thoughts of a normal and happy family life down from the shelf and use them to encourage myself that one day I would indeed have that kind of life. For now, I was on a roller-coaster ride, and there seemed to be no way to get off.

When we start looking for things to spend money on, they have a way of appearing miraculously. It did not take long for me to learn that there are a lot of ways a man can be separated from his money. I quickly discovered the local night scene, where anything I wanted could be bought for a price. The life I wanted was for sale, and I was buying!

There had been drugs in my hometown, but nothing like the scale I was now introduced to. If you knew the right people and had enough money, any kind of drug could be found.

I learned another funny thing about money. When you have it, everybody wants to be your friend, and when you don't, you find out who your friends really are. At the moment, I had it, and the atmosphere in the eighties was very conducive to drug use, so I had plenty of friends. Everyone I knew enjoyed some type of drug on a social level. It was quite socially acceptable to use drugs, just as long as you knew your limitations and kept your drug intake at a level that did not exceed your income.

One of the greatest misconceptions people have about drug users is that they are all down-and-outers living in the street, unable to function. Nothing could be further from the truth. Drugs permeate every level of American society. While there are many drug users who are living as down-and-outers, all the people I knew during this period of my life were professionals who were up-and-coming, successful business people.

I jumped into my new lifestyle with both feet, and I seemed to be right at home. With money in my pocket and plenty of spending opportunities available to me, I was having the time of my life. I congratulated myself often for the smart choice I had made to seek my fortune in the world.

While I was riding high on this crest of financial success, I had another door open to me that showed promise of further increasing my income and my social status. My colleagues and I were hired by a large company to train their employees. Because this new position promised bigger and better opportunities for success, I willingly made a move to Atlantic Beach, North Carolina, to accommodate it.

It took me about a year to learn the ropes of my new career, but it eventually started to pay off. By nature I have a lot of drive to accomplish what I have started. God designed me that way. To this day I don't like to waste time or leave a project unfinished, and this character trait served me well and helped me move higher on the ladder of success.

By 1982, I was being driven by my desire for financial success, and helping to fuel my drive was an expensive white powder I was becoming increasingly more dependent upon. What at first was an exciting high, that seemingly enabled me to have almost superhuman powers of boundless energy and animation, soon became a harsh taskmaster. This master demanded that I take more and more cocaine to achieve results that no longer fueled my drive to succeed but rather fed my physical addiction.

It was an endless cycle. The addiction started so insidiously that I didn't realize how far I had gone until it was almost too late.

During my stay in Atlantic Beach, North Carolina, I met Beverly, the woman who would become my wife. When we met, she was still in college and was working part-time in a private club that I began to frequent. When we first met, I asked her out on a date, but she told me she couldn't go because she was seeing someone else. I realize now that it wasn't God's timing for us to develop a relationship when we first met.

Besides working in the club, Beverly also had a catering business. However, her real source of income was transporting cocaine. She was a drug dealer.

Over the years I have often told my testimony of being a drug user and Beverly being a drug dealer, and I have shared that it was a great combination. In reality, Beverly was trying to put that lifestyle behind her when we met.

In the first chapter, I assured you that God is everywhere you are. Let me remind you that the psalmist said:

If I ascend up into heaven, thou art there: if I make my bed in hell,
behold, thou art there.   Psalm 139:8

It is true. I had begun my descent into Hell, but even there God was orchestrating my life and directing my path.

After a while, I moved to another part of North Carolina. I was working my way back to South Carolina where I had started. For the moment Beverly and I were on two very different paths. Despite my growing dependence on drugs, I was still very successful and would continue to be successful until something quite remarkable happened. Beverly was on another track altogether, and her double life was about to catch up with her.

We had only met that once, and nothing had come of it. A year or so later I was living in a completely different city, still pursuing success and recognition, but Beverly was about to have an encounter with an undercover drug agent that would change her life forever. In May of 1984 she was arrested for giving away an illegal substance. Because she had not sold the drug, she was put on probation rather than being jailed. It was enough to make her take a long, hard look at her life and make the decision to get out of the drug business.

In July of that year, I went back to Atlantic Beach for a sales meeting. One night I went to the same club where I had first met Beverly, and to my surprise, I ran into her again. This time she was there as a patron, not on business. Looking back on the experience later, it seemed to both of us that she had been there waiting for me. When I saw her, I walked right over to her, and from that moment to this we have been together. God was leading and guiding me to my future wife, even though neither one of us was serving Him at the time. How great is His mercy!

What happened next is so incredible that each time I retell the story I cannot help but give God glory for His amazing grace. As we parted company that first night, Beverly and I made plans for a date the next day. When we met, we began to smoke marijuana and drink beer as we got to know each other over lunch. Before we knew it, lunch had turned into dinner, and we had switched from beer to wine.

As we sat across the table from one another, Beverly looked at me and said, "You know, you're going to be a preacher one day." I thought to myself, *You sure are pretty, but you are the craziest chick I have ever met!* I had no way of knowing what had prompted her to say such a thing. She later told me that two years prior to this she had been on a drug run, with eight ounces of cocaine in her car on a back road in the wee hours of the morning, when it seemed as though she had pulled into a drive-in theatre. The very skies seemed to open up to her, and she saw herself standing beside a tall man with black hair. Both she and the man had microphones in their hands, and they were ministering to what looked like an ocean of people stretching in all directions as far as the eye could see.

She did not presently have a relationship with Jesus, although she, like me, had accepted Him as her Savior when she was a small child. Although she knew nothing about the indwelling of the Holy Spirit, she somehow knew that God was showing her what His plan for her future was. She spoke out loud in her car that morning and told God that He had the wrong woman. Inside of her, she felt she heard God chuckle, as if to say, "We'll see about that!"

At this time in her life, Beverly did not yet understand what it meant to maintain a relationship with Christ, yet God's faithfulness to make sure the Holy Spirit kept her and guided her was manifesting itself. What happened to her that day had nothing to do with her behavior or her lifestyle. It happened only because of the grace of God. The Holy Spirit is not afraid of darkness and will go with us wherever He has to, to make sure we make it back to Jesus. Paul wrote to the Ephesians:

> *...that ye, being rooted and grounded in love, may be able to comprehend with all saints what is the breadth, and length, and depth, and height; and to know the love of Christ, which passeth knowledge, that ye might be filled with all the fulness of God.*   Ephesians 3:17-19

From the moment Beverly confessed with her mouth that I was going to be a preacher, everything in my life, in the natural, began to fall apart. This, too, was of God.

I did not know it at the time, but my brother, who has been a pastor for twenty-six years, had been led to change the way he prayed for me. Although he knew the kind of lifestyle I was living, he had always prayed that God would keep me and bless me. Around this same time he had started asking God to do WHATEVER IT TOOK, short of killing me, to bring me into the Kingdom.

God was working to fulfill my destiny, although I had willfully walked away from Him. Sometimes, in order to take us to the mountaintop, God has to allow us to go through the valley. In my experience I have learned that I can shorten my stay in the valley through obedience or I can lengthen it through disobedience.

Not really understanding at the time that God was wooing me by His Holy Spirit, the only real change I made in my life was to make Beverly my wife and move her and her son Josh to the city where I lived. Everything else continued on much as before.

Two years passed after Beverly told me I was going to be a preacher, and I had become more entrenched in the drug culture than ever, twice overdosing on cocaine. The drug use also took its toll on my finances. I was now more in debt than I had ever been in my life. I would lie awake in bed at night with the full knowledge that my life was falling apart, but I seemed helpless to do anything about it. I would ask Beverly, "Is it time yet?"

Her response was always the same, "That's between you and God."

I thought that if I could change my geographical location I might be able to make a change in the way I was living. Drugs were too readily available to me. Although Beverly had gotten out of the drug business and moved away from her drug connections, I had made my own contacts, and the drugs would appear as if by magic. One night we came home to find a note on the kitchen table. It said, "The stash is in your kitchen cupboard."

Sure enough, we opened the door, and there was a half-pound of cocaine. This happened a number of times, so although I had thoughts of somehow getting out, I was getting in deeper all the time.

What was worse, I was endangering not only Beverly and myself but also our nine-year-old son, Josh. I packed up Beverly and Josh and left for Virginia Beach, Virginia. I was determined to make a fresh start with a new company, and I hoped I could get my feet back on the ground in the process.

While we were living in Virginia Beach, my parents came for a visit, and during their stay I collapsed in front of them. They packed me into their car and took me to an emergency room. From there I was taken back to Alabama, where I spent two weeks in a hospital under the watchful eyes of my family and their doctor. The diagnosis was that I was a drugged-out, stressed-out, sick young man, and if I didn't get off of the drugs and pull myself together, I was going to die.

I knew two things about dying, having gleaned this information from my years spent in church as a child. The first piece of information that came to mind was that Heaven and Hell are real places. The second piece of information was that if you were good, you would go to Heaven, and if you were not, you would go to Hell. I knew I would never qualify for Heaven unless something really radical happened, so soon after I was released from the hospital I went to church one night.

As the evangelist started to preach, I felt as though a physical hand had taken hold of my heart and was squeezing it. I quickly came to the conclusion that I was having a heart attack and started begging God for the young man to stop preaching and make the altar call so that I could make my way to the altar and ask Jesus to forgive me of my sins. I was desperate to accept Him as Lord of my life. It never occurred to me that I could have prayed right there where I was seated.

I cannot tell you what the evangelist said that night. This lets me know that, as important as we preachers think we are, we really have nothing to do with this matter of the salvation of souls. We are just the messengers. It is the Holy Spirit who does the work.

As I sat there, begging God to save me, the young man stopped preaching and walked right to the fourth row where I was sitting. He took me by the hand and said, "It's time you got right with God!"

I agreed and replied, "Yes, it is!"

It was a Spirit-filled church, and six men promptly swarmed around me like bees. Three of them were saying, "Hang on," and the other three were saying, "Let go!" I didn't know if I should "hang on" or "let go." Aside from that, I could not tell you what else they said or what I said, but I can say that in about fifteen minutes I got up, and I was FREE! I had been completely delivered from drug addiction and have never had the desire for drugs or alcohol since that night. I left the church completely delivered from the bondage of drug addiction, and my spirit was soaring like an eagle.

After my release from the hospital, Bev and Josh had joined me in Alabama. My parents had sold their home and were temporarily living with my sister Brenda and her family. Bev and Josh were there too, and I went straight there to tell Bev I had been saved. Her reaction was not the one I was hoping for.

To this day, I'm not sure that it was ever discussed with Brenda that we, too, would be moving into her house for an indefinite stay. Even though it was a good-sized home, there were three families now living under one roof. Altogether there were ten of us. Because of that experience, I understand why the Bible instructs children to leave their parents and cleave to their mates (see Genesis 2:24). The circumstances of living with so many in those cramped quarters may have influenced Bev's response to my announcement about being saved. She said she didn't really care what had happened to me. She no longer wanted any part of what I was doing, and she was ready to leave Alabama.

A few days later, Bev relented and agreed to attend a church service with me. She had never been in a Spirit-filled service before, and it was a little intimidating for her. The louder the music got, the closer she held Josh to herself. At one point, she was so disturbed by the proceedings that she promised Josh that the two of them would get out of there alive.

After that experience, Bev was convinced that I had lost my mind. I was desperately praying for her to be saved, "God," I prayed, "save Bev. If You can do it for me, You can do it for her!" This went on for several weeks without any hint that the Lord was hearing or answering.

Tempers were growing shorter each day as we all tried to coexist in the same house. Finally, on one midwinter night Beverly decided that she had to get away from there, at least for a while. As she pulled off from the house she dug around in the car ashtray until she found a marijuana cigarette, and while she was smoking it, she heard the voice of the Lord asking her what she was doing digging around in that trash. He said, "Now is the time; come unto Me, My child!" God invited her into His Kingdom in the middle of her smoking a joint!

As soon as Bev heard God's voice, wave after wave of pure love began to flood over her. She was so overcome by the power of God that she had to pull off to the side of the road to compose herself. She still doesn't remember how long she was there or what she said to the Lord, but by the time she had made her way back home she had accepted Jesus as her Lord and Savior.

She ran into the house, tears streaming down her face, and I feared that she had been in an accident. As she began to pour her heart out to me, telling me that we just had to go to church and we had to go right then, I began to understand that God had miraculously saved my wife in the front seat of her car.

That was the first of many answered prayers for me. Although I had reached one of the lowest points in my life, God had never left me. He had not forsaken me. He literally went to the pit of Hell and rescued me.

No matter how high, no matter how low, no matter how far from God you have gone, HE IS THERE.

Ultimately, we have the peace of knowing that it is not our responsibility to find our destiny. It is the Good Shepherd who will lead and guide us. All we have to do is follow His lead! While being guided to the High Places in God, our journey is made much easier if we just obey!

Chapter 3

Guided by an Unseen Hand

The Spirit of Truth ... will guide you into all Truth.   John 16:13

After such radical conversions, I think it would be fair to say that we were both shell-shocked. We still didn't know where we were going to live, how we were going to support ourselves, and, quite literally, where our next meal would come from. The only thing we were confident of was that God had removed us from the life we had known, and there would be no going back.

Almost immediately I started receiving calls from the company I had started with, asking me to come back. They offered me a house, a car, better benefits, a promotion — "anything," they said, "just come back." Beverly's opinion was that I should take the job. After all, we could serve God anywhere. In the natural, that seemed like the sensible thing to do, but already the Holy Spirit was guiding me to my destiny.

I wasn't aware at the time that the urging deep inside me was the Holy Spirit at work, and I would not figure that out until much later. All I knew at the time was that I would be making the biggest mistake of my life if I went back to what God had just de-livered me from.

It still amazes me that the same Holy Spirit who brought me back to Jesus would lead me and that He had literally been as-

39

signed by Jesus Himself to direct my path. Who better could lead us than the Spirit of God? Who knows the mind and will of God better than the Spirit of God Himself?

Jesus made it very clear what the Holy Spirit's intentions are:

Howbeit when he, the Spirit of Truth, is come, he will guide you into all truth: for he shall not speak of himself; but whatsoever he shall hear, that shall he speak: and he will shew you things to come. John 16:13

The Lord was preparing me for the future He had planned for me all along. In the years to come, as I began to study the Word of God, I came to understand a bit of how Abram must have felt when God spoke to him:

Now the LORD had said unto Abram, Get thee out of thy country, and from thy kindred, and from thy father's house, unto a land that I will shew thee. Genesis 12:1

Trying to explain to my own family that I could not go back to my former career, no matter how great the incentives were, was difficult — to say the least. My position just did not make sense to them.

Abram must have had the same problem. In his day there were gods for everything. Trying to explain to his family that GOD had spoken to him to take all his possessions and leave home in search of some unknown land must have been difficult. I can imagine that his father might have said something like: "Abram, if you could just tell me *which* god spoke to you, perhaps I would understand your determination to leave home!"

Fortunately, Abram possessed a faith that was great enough to carry him and his entire family into an unknown land. I knew nothing about faith or trusting God. All I knew was that I could not go back. I still didn't know where I would go, but I was sure God would go with me.

It might have been different if God had spoken to Abram on a daily basis to encourage him, but there were years between the times he heard from God. Even though I am sure Abram sought God daily and communed with Him, the Word of God is clear that Abram had to stand on what God had already spoken to him, as he moved his family from place to place. During the silent times his faith had to sustain him (see Genesis 12-17). Although I was not yet sure what God's plan was, I did have the knowledge that the Spirit of God had come to abide in me and that I was being guided by an unseen hand. It was imperative that I remain obedient to what I believed to be God leading me.

God's Spirit also led the children of Israel. Nehemiah wrote:

Thou gavest also thy good spirit to instruct them.   Nehemiah 9:20

As they were leaving Egypt the Israelites were met by a cloud by day and a fire by night, and this visible presence of God guided them on their journey. I used to think that when God did these miracles He was only demonstrating His supernatural capabilities. Then I traveled to and climbed Mount Sinai. When we started our climb in the early morning hours it was freezing cold, with temperatures in the twenties. By mid-morning we were burning up, as the temperatures reached into the high nineties. God is a practical God. During the day He provided air-conditioning for His people, and at night He supplied them with heat.

The Holy Spirit was leading, guiding and protecting me, even though I was like the man described by Jesus in John 14:17:

Even the Spirit of truth; whom the world cannot receive, because it

seeth him not, neither knoweth him: but ye know him; for he dwelleth
with you, and shall be in you. John 14:17

I had just come out of the world and was not at all familiar with
God's way of doing things, but I was very much aware that I was
being guided by an invisible strength coming from the very
depths of my being. We would not have said in those days that
God's Spirit was guiding us, but we had no liberty to go back to
the world (Egypt). We also had no clear direction on what to do
about the future.

I have since learned that the Holy Spirit leads us with an inner
witness. When a wrong decision is about to be made, we have no
peace about it. With clear direction comes the peace of God:

For ye shall go out with joy, and be led forth with peace. Isaiah 55:12

Waiting for clear direction was a problem for me, and it still is.
I have no problem with the faith part of waiting for God to answer, but the patience part is something I am still working on.
This was my first learning experience in waiting on God. Since
that time I have learned that God usually answers in one of these
ways: YES, NO, WAIT, or YOU'VE GOT TO BE KIDDING! When
the answer is WAIT, it is often because He wants to do something
in our lives and desires for us to come into a closer relationship
with Him.

At times we may seem to be going in circles, with no clear direction at all. Then, without warning, a circumstance will present
itself that will change everything. This is exactly how I felt during the early period of my Christian life. It seemed as though
every avenue was supernaturally blocked, and I had no idea of
the direction I was to take or how situations would change. Little
did I know that God had already arranged things for me:

For I know the plans I have for you, says the Lord. They are plans for
good and not for evil, to give you a future and a hope.
                                                    Jeremiah 29:11, TLB

My *"hope"* came in the form of an offer extended to us by my
parents, to move to Orlando, Florida. They had invested in some
property there and had developed several parcels of it. They
were moving there and invited us to join them until we got back
on our feet. At the time, the move didn't seem very important. I
looked at it as a reprieve, a little more time to hear from God and
get clear direction for my life. Beverly and I made the decision to
go, and for the first time in many months I experienced real
peace. What seemed like a trivial matter at the time would
change my entire life.

Guided by an unseen hand and still unaware of it, we headed
to Orlando, arriving on the evening of February 21, 1987. I knew
only one person in the greater Orlando area. The man was a
former employee and friend that I had smoked marijuana with
on many occasions. As soon as we got settled in, I gave him a call
to let him know we were in town. He was delighted to hear from
me. The first question out of his mouth was, "Do you have any
pot?"

I told him that I had been born again and no longer did drugs.
He didn't seem at all surprised. He stated matter-of-factly that
the same thing had happened to his wife, and he invited us to
join them for church the next day. He told me the music was
great in the church they were attending and that real miracles
happened there. He went on to say that the place was packed
with people who waited in line for hours to get into the service.

Excitedly, he shared that all of the ushers wore red jackets. He
had a red jacket, and he planned to pretend to be an usher so that
he could get us good seats. I told him that wasn't necessary, but

sure enough, the next day he showed up wearing a bright red blazer. We sat on the fourth row, front and center. By then we knew the name of the pastor of the church. He was Pastor Benny Hinn.

How ironic that my relationship with a drug abuser should lead me to the church where I would receive the foundation for my journey to the High Places! God is a radical God. He is the Creator of everything. He truly uses *"the foolish things ... to confound the wise"* (1 Corinthians 1:27). If God could use Balaam's donkey to speak truth into the prophet's life, surely He can use a drug abuser or anyone else He chooses to reach out to us (see Numbers 22: 23-31).

Since beginning my journey to the High Places, I have been told by many sincere believers to be careful and not miss God. Personally, I have come to believe that GOD IS TOO BIG TO MISS. The Bible says that Heaven and Earth cannot contain Him. Even when you fail, God will not allow you to miss Him. He is always there, waiting for you to return to Him. No matter how high or how low you have gone, He is there!

If you have not gotten answers to questions about your ultimate destiny, it may be because God is drawing you into a deeper relationship with Himself and, very possibly, leading you in a completely different direction than you were originally headed. The psalmist declared:

> *The Lord is my shepherd; I shall not want.*   Psalm 23:1

I have come to understand that sheep really are some of the dumbest of God's creatures. There can be food and water right in front of them or just over the hill, but they will not find it unless they have a shepherd to lead them.

Sheep are very dependent upon their shepherd, and they will

go without unless they have a shepherd who is committed to caring for them. It is not because of their own ability to follow that they survive. It is because of the shepherd's ability to lead.

Ultimately, we have the peace of knowing that it is not our responsibility to find our destiny. It is the Good Shepherd who will lead and guide us into it. All we must do is follow His lead. This simple obedience is crucial. While being guided to the High Places in God, our journey is made so much easier if we just obey Him at every juncture.

The church we were led to that winter's day was Orlando Christian Center. We had never experienced the presence of God as it was manifested there. It was flowing through that ministry like a great river, and all we had to do was jump in.

That morning, as we sat under the incredible teaching of Pastor Benny Hinn for the first time, we had no idea what an important part he would play in the journey upon which we had embarked. I think I understand now why God keeps His plans for His children to Himself. If He had told me then what the next ten years of my life would hold, I would never have believed it.

Jeremiah promised:

His plans for you are good plans, to give you a future and a hope.
Jeremiah 29:11

My future in God was just beginning, but His unseen hand was lovingly shaping my journey to the High Places.

God's first covenant with His people set a standard, but the shed blood of Jesus established His grace and opened the door to our hearts for intimacy with our Creator.

CHAPTER 4

YOU HAVE ALL ACCESS

For through Him [Christ Jesus] we both have access by one Spirit unto
the Father.   Ephesians 2:18

Before we go any further, I feel it is necessary to lay a proper
foundation for climbing. Before a climber proceeds higher, he
must have a solid foundation from which to step. The Word of
God states:

Be not carried about with divers and strange doctrines: for it is a good
thing that the heart be established with grace; not with meats, which
have not profited them that have been occupied therein.
                                                               Hebrews 13:9

It is God's grace and His grace alone that allows our pursuit to
continue to the High Places. Jesus is both *"the author"* and *"[the]*
finisher of our faith" (Hebrews 12:2). It is by His grace that we can
begin the climb, and it is only by His grace that we can finish.
Because of the work of the cross, each and every one of us, regardless of our culture, race, creed or gender, has access to the
High Places in God through the blood of the New Covenant.

When Moses came down from the mountaintop with instructions to build the Tabernacle, God told him:

See that you make all things according to the pattern shown you on the mountain. Hebrews 8:5, NKJ

The Tabernacle was a shadow of the work of the cross:

... He has obtained a more excellent ministry, inasmuch as He is also Mediator of a better covenant, which was established on better promises. For if that first covenant had been faultless, then no place would have been sought for a second. Verses 6-7, NKJ

God's first covenant with His people set a standard, but the shed blood of Jesus established His grace and opened the door to our hearts for intimacy with our Creator. The writer of Hebrews continued:

For this is the covenant that I will make with the house of Israel after those days, says the LORD: I will put My laws in their mind and write them on their hearts; and I will be their God, and they shall be My people. Hebrews 8:10, NKJ

Grace and mercy are the standards for the New Covenant. In this New Covenant we are being drawn by the Holy Spirit into a personal relationship with God. His New Covenant is now in the minds and hearts of those who believe, by His Spirit. This work is established from the inside out, not the outside in. There is immediate and total access to the knowledge of God and to an intimate relationship with God, through the Spirit.

Early in my Christian walk I struggled with understanding the unmerited grace and love of God. Just as a pendulum swings, I went far to one side, trying to make myself pleasing to God and worthy of His love. If I didn't read my Bible a certain amount of time, I allowed myself to come under condemnation. My prayer time had to be strictly regimented, and I spent countless hours volunteering my time for church functions. There is nothing wrong with any of these activities. In fact, each one of them is very important. The problem was my motivation. Our human instincts (the soulish realm and sin nature) tell us that we must earn everything we get. However, God says that Jesus has earned this privilege for us and that all we have to do is accept the privilege — by faith.

In the book of Romans, Paul shows us:

> *Therefore, having been justified by faith, we have peace with God through our Lord Jesus Christ, through whom also we have access by faith into this grace in which we stand, and rejoice in hope of the glory of God.* Romans 5:1-2, NKJ

In the book of Ephesians he states:

> *For through Him we both have access by one Spirit to the Father.* Ephesians 2:18, NKJ

It is not our prayer life, our Bible devotions, our church attendance or any other religious activity that gives us the right to approach God and walk in His presence. It is only through the blood of Jesus His Son that we have this right.

The Holy Spirit of God has sealed us and has given us all access. The privilege we enjoy is much like a person who has a backstage pass at a concert, sporting event or convention. That pass declares "all access," and the person wearing it can go anywhere he chooses. In the same way we as believers have this same privilege because of being sealed with the Holy Spirit. Once we are sealed with the Holy Spirit, we have access through the Spirit to all that God has for us in the High Places.

As believers we sometimes put limitations on the plans and purposes God has for us. His desire is for us to have access to all that He has for us in this life and for all eternity. It is because of our relationship with our heavenly Father, through the work of the cross and the indwelling Holy Spirit, that every good and perfect thing God has planned for us can be accessed. The shed blood of Jesus Christ assures our entry into the very presence of God.

Jesus said that He is *"the Way, the Truth and the Life"* (John 14:6). He has given us access to the very throne of God. To illustrate this point of grace, I would like to briefly expound on a vast subject — the Tabernacle of Moses, for the Tabernacle was a perfect shadow, or example, of our entrance into God's presence through grace.

In the Old Covenant, only one man (the High Priest) was allowed to enter the Holy of Holies, and he could do it just once a year. He went there to make an atonement for the sins of the children of Israel. No one else was privileged to enter in this way into God's presence.

With this privilege came great responsibility. If the High Priest had not followed the proper instructions concerning sacrifice and purification, or if he had sin in his life, he would be struck dead because of it. Fully aware of this fact, he approached the throne of God's judgment in great fear every time that time of year rolled around.

In the approach to the wilderness Tabernacle there was a wonderful spiritual image of Christ. The gate, which was the entrance of the Outer Court, was called the Way. It was made of purple, scarlet, white and blue material. The purple spoke of Jesus, the King of kings. The scarlet represented Jesus, the suffering Savior. The white represented Jesus, the Son of God. And the blue represented Jesus, the Son of Man.

As one entered the Holy Place, or Inner Court, there were five pillars that held the dividing curtain. This entrance was called Truth. Truth represents the fivefold ministries of the church that together reveal the Truth of God to us.

As one entered the Holy of Holies, there was a veil that was called Life, for behind the veil was the presence of the Creator, the Most High God, the Giver of life itself. It was His presence that made that section of the Tabernacle the Most High, or Most Holy, Place.

These three attributes, the Way, the Truth and the Life, were exactly what Jesus said He was:

Jesus saith unto him, I am the way, the truth, and the life.

John 14:6

He is the Way into God's presence, He is the Truth about God's presence, and He is the Life of God's presence.

Inside the Holy of Holies the Ark of the Covenant was kept. It was a box, the dimensions of which are found in Exodus 25:10. The Bible tells us some very interesting facts about the Ark of the Covenant.

Hebrews 9:4 declares that the Ark contained a golden pot full of manna from the wilderness, Aaron's rod which budded and the tablets on which the Ten Commandments were written. Each of these elements speaks of a time in which Israel was in rebellion. In Exodus 16:2 we see Israel murmuring against Moses and Aaron because of their hunger. God answered with bread from Heaven, the manna. This still did not satisfy them, and in Numbers 11 we see the people of Israel rebelling against manna and lusting after flesh. In response, God sent them quail. In Numbers 16 we see Korah leading Israel in rebellion against Moses and

Aaron. As a result, a plague came upon Israel, and ultimately, in Chapter 17, God said to Moses:

> *Speak unto the children of Israel, and take of every one of them a rod according to the house of their fathers, of all their princes according to the house of their fathers, twelve rods: write thou every man's name upon his rod.*　　　　　　　Numbers 17:2

God told Moses to lay these rods in the Tabernacle and that He would use them to give a sign. The rod that budded would reveal which tribe had His favor. In addition, God said that He would cause the murmuring to stop:

> *The rod of Aaron for the house of Levi was budded, and brought forth buds, and bloomed blossoms, and yielded almonds.*　　Numbers 17:8

God then commanded that they keep that rod as a *"token against the rebels"*:

> *And the Lord said unto Moses, Bring Aaron's rod before the testimony, to be kept for a token against the rebels; and thou shalt quite take away their murmurings from me, that they die not.*　　Numbers 17:10

After God gave Moses the Ten Commandments, he carried the tablets down the mountain to present to the people, only to find them in idol worship before a golden calf they had created (see Exodus 32 to 34). Grieved, Moses broke the tablets, and judgment came upon the idolaters. It is interesting to note what the Bible gives as the reason the people took such rash action. It was because Moses stayed longer than they expected on the mountain. Coming to the conclusion that he was never coming back led them to return to idol worship. In times when we are believing and trusting God, we must be willing to wait patiently for Him. If we refuse to do so, we can move ahead of God and into idolatry. The good news is that God in His infinite mercy and grace is still right there waiting for you to once again turn from your rebellion and idolatry to His salvation. Even though the Israelites in their impatience turned to idol worship, God forgave them and called Moses to His holy mountain and gave him the commandments for the second time.

Each of these items, as we have seen — the manna, the rod of Aaron and the tablets of stone — represented rebellion, sin and idolatry. God commanded these signs of rebellion to be placed in a wooden box and the box to be covered with gold. Wood speaks of humanity, and gold speaks of divinity — Jesus the Son of Man and Jesus the Son of God combined to bring us salvation from our rebellion. It was over the Ark that the Mercy Seat rested, and it was here that God chose to dwell. His presence was over top of our sin and rebellion.

It was there on the Mercy Seat that once a year the blood of sacrificial animals was to be applied. The Mercy Seat represented God's judgment, and therefore it was required, without fail, that the High Priest apply to it the blood of an animal slain as an atonement for the sins of the people. As we have seen, this was serious business, for if the priest himself was not properly atoned for before he entered this Most Holy Place, he would instantly be struck dead by the holy presence of God and would have to be dragged out by a rope attached to his ankle. As we can imagine, this produced much fear and trembling in the priests who were forced to do the dragging.

The good news is that Jesus Christ of Nazareth has become our great High Priest and has once and for all made the proper atonement for our sins (see Hebrews 10:10). This atonement was not made with the blood of an animal, but with His own blood (see

Hebrews 13:12). He entered the Holy of Holies and applied His own blood over our sin and rebellion and thus made atonement for all mankind — for all time.

In doing this, Jesus turned a throne of judgment into a throne of grace (see Hebrews 4:16). Now we can come to God through *"a new and living way"* (Hebrews 10:20). We need not come with fear, but with liberty. Hallelujah! We have no reason to fear death as we approach God's presence.

We are already *"dead in trespasses and sins"* (Ephesians 2:1), but Jesus is our anchor of hope (see Hebrews 6:19). He entered in before us and prepared the way. He is now seated at the right hand of God as our faithful heavenly High Priest.

As our High Priest, Jesus pulls us into God's presence, and He does it with His love. Though we are dead, we receive life, and we come out whole by God's grace and power. In the Old Covenant the priest went in alive and was dragged out dead because of sin. In the New Covenant we are dragged in dead in our sin and trespasses, and we come out alive because of the righteousness of God in Christ Jesus.

As we climb to higher heights, we must never lose sight of the fact that, even at these higher heights of spiritual maturity, our righteousness is still as filthy rags before God. His grace given to us through Jesus Christ is our only means of access, never our own abilities. To Him be glory forever!

At times, I believe, the works of righteousness we try to create in ourselves are rooted and grounded in pride. We think that our works are something we can do to obtain God's favor. To enter into God's presence, however, or to go to the High Places, we must trust in what Jesus has done for us. That alone is what gives us access to the very throne of God. It is known, therefore, as a throne of grace, not a throne of works. The Bible shows us that we are seated *"together in heavenly places in Christ Jesus"* (Ephesians 2:6). Christ has provided us access to the heavenly places through His throne of grace.

After I got saved and began to follow the Lord and to climb to the High Places, I experienced the pendulum effect I mentioned earlier in this chapter. I went from being a drug addict, far from the knowledge of Christ, to being a religious fanatic who thought I knew everything about serving God. I left the baggage of my former life far behind, only to pick up the yoke of religious bondage. I would spend hours praying, and then when I came out of my prayer closet and found my family watching a harmless sitcom like *I Love Lucy,* I would shout at them to turn it off. "That's of the devil," I would tell them.

I got so fanatic that I think Beverly wanted to *turn me off* about that time. I would not permit any deviled eggs or devil's food cake to come into our home. I delighted in smashing anything I thought might be or might conceivably become an idol. I went to great extremes.

One day Pastor Benny shared a story with us. While preaching at a conference, he had met David DuPlessis in one of the hallways outside. He excitedly asked Brother DuPlessis how he could be more pleasing to God, and eagerly he awaited the answer. David DuPlessis turned to him, put his finger into his chest, and said, "Don't even try to please God. It is not your ability, but His ability in you." With that, he said "Good night" and left without another word. Pastor Benny later told me that it has taken him more than twenty years to understand what David DuPlessis meant.

Many people become frustrated serving God because they have their faith in faith, not in God. Faith in faith is believing that it is our responsibility to please God, when, in reality, it is our response to His ability that pleases Him.

It is only by God's mercy and grace that we can continue the climb of faith. What God requires of us is to keep our hearts stayed on Him and to continually look up to Him, trusting that He will be there — even when we stumble and fall.

The call of God is the call from *God to fulfill your purpose on this Earth.*

CHAPTER 5

PRESSING TOWARD
THE HIGH CALL OF GOD

Brethren, I count not myself to have apprehended: but this one thing I
do, forgetting those things which are behind, and reaching forth unto
those things which are before, I press toward the mark for the prize of
the HIGH CALLING OF GOD in Christ Jesus.

Philippians 3:13-14

I believe the High Call of God is the will of God, and fulfilling the will of God is not just for a pastor, an evangelist, a prophet, an apostle or a teacher. Fulfilling God's call for your life — which may be to become a housewife, a businessman, a schoolteacher or whatever your life description may be, as a ministry unto the Lord — is fulfilling the High Call of God. Doing whatever you do and having His presence go with you is answering the High Call.

Whether you are called to be a preacher, a businessman, a schoolteacher, a mechanic, a housewife or any other occupation, you are walking in your calling as long as you are obedient to what God has asked of you. He has placed you right where you are, to tell those who are in your life about His Son Jesus and what He has done for you.

God's plan is perfect, and everything you have been through

up to this point in your life has simply been preparation preceding walking in His High Call.

The call of God is the call FROM God to fulfill your purpose on this Earth. The will of God is not always instantly found, and I have come to believe that we learn it gradually, over time. The Scriptures teach:

> *That you may prove what is that good and acceptable and perfect will of God.*   Romans 12:2, NKJ

We begin in the *"good"* will of God, move to the *"acceptable"* will of God, and finally come into the *"perfect"* will of God for our lives. Throughout this progression we have the promise that He will work out His plans for our lives (see Hebrews 13:20-21).

God first places a desire in your heart, and then He gives you your heart's desire. I remember that when I was a small boy I sometimes put on my Sunday suit during the week and pretended that I was a preacher. I believe that God was sowing a seed in me for the future. For some, it may be a desire to become a doctor or a lawyer or some other career choice.

The call of God came to me in a rather unusual way. After attending Pastor Benny's church in Orlando that first time with my pot-smoking friend, we made it our home church. It was then, and it still is today, a large church with some two thousand in attendance at every service. Even after we had attended for several months, we still knew very few people personally because of the vastness of the crowds.

One Sunday night Beverly and I were sitting on the left side of the sanctuary, about three-quarters of the way back. There was a big crowd, as usual. During the worship service I prayed a prayer straight from my heart. I said to God, "If You want to use me for Your service, just let me know. I'll do anything! If You don't want to place me in ministry, I will serve You anyway, in whatever capacity. But if You want me to do something specific that I am not already doing, just let me know."

Not more than sixty seconds after I had uttered these words to the Lord, Pastor Benny stopped preaching, pointed right at Beverly and me, and said, "Young man, come up here and bring your wife." We looked around, wondering whom he was speaking to, and when we finally realized it was us, I was dumbfounded. I thought, *God cannot be this real.* I had just prayed, and sixty seconds later He was answering.

We approached the platform hesitantly, and as we did, Pastor Benny opened his mouth and began to speak by the oracles of God:

> *I've called you by name, and you are Mine. The trials of the past have come to an end, and the glories of tomorrow shall be revealed to you in clarity.*
> *Be not dismayed, for I am thy God. I will help you, yea, I will uphold you with the right hand of My righteousness.*
> *Be faithful, be strong. Be strong, for I will cause wounded lambs to come your way, and you will pick them up in your arms, not only pick them up, but yes, deliver them from the hands of the oppressor. I shall place thee in a place of ministry. I will place you in a ministry, not only picking up lambs and bringing deliverance from the oppressor, but also strengthening them and seeing them grow.*
> *No, thy days are not finished. Your dream is not over, for they that know Me shall do exploits and shall be strong. I again remind you My call is on your life. My ministry for you will come, and nothing, nothing shall keep Me from accomplishing it!*

The power of God came upon the two of us so strongly that Beverly literally crumbled in the presence of God. After it was over, we made our way back to our seats, still numb from what had just happened. No sooner had we gotten back to our seats than Pastor Benny stopped his preaching again. "Young man," he said, looking my way, "stand up again."

I thought, *My God, what's going to happen now?*

He looked at me intensely and said, "I don't know how or when, but I know God is going to place you in ministry ... in this church ... with me."

You have to get the picture. Here was an ex-drug dealer and an ex-drug addict who had absolutely no theological training, and God was calling us, not only to enter the ministry, but to work with Pastor Benny Hinn. Beverly, at least, had a college education, but I had only finished high school. (Since the high school I attended in Alabama was called Oxford High, I tell the people around the world who ask me where I received my education, "Oxford," and I leave it at that.) Needless to say, we felt less than qualified to be in the ministry. We were learning, however, that God sometimes uses foolish things *"to confound the wise"* (1 Corinthians 1:27).

After this powerful prophecy, I began to press into God like never before. Every time there was a service, I was there. I studied my Bible, I prayed, I fasted. I wanted what God had for me. I can relate to what the Apostle Paul said to the Philippians:

> *Not that I have already attained, or am already perfected; but I press on, that I may lay hold of that for which Christ Jesus has also laid hold of me. Brethren, I do not count myself to have apprehended; but one thing I do, forgetting those things which are behind and reaching forward to those things which are ahead.* Philippians 3:12-13, NKJ

When writing to Timothy, he showed that we must press into the things of God that are ahead and *"lay hold on"* them:

Pressing Toward the High Call of God

Fight the good fight of faith, lay hold on eternal life. 1 Timothy 6:12

Jesus said:

The kingdom of God is preached, and every man presseth into it.
Luke 16:16

The message is clear. When the will of God is revealed to us about our future or destiny, we must press in. Just because it is revealed or spoken does not necessarily make it come to pass. God promised the people of Israel that they would enter the land of Canaan, yet the generation God delivered from Egypt died in the wilderness and never made it in because of their rebellion (see Numbers 26:64-65). Although God had the Promised Land prepared for them, it was the next generation that entered in.

It is important that we pursue God, laying hold of what He has for us, and pressing into the High Call of God in Christ Jesus. We must set aside every weight (sin and rebellion) that is holding us back from answering His call and walking in the High Places (see Hebrews 12:1-2).

We all go through what I call the wilderness of waiting. I mentioned it already in Chapter 3. It is the time between the promise and its fulfillment. Paul warned every believer that we must not be overthrown in the wilderness (see 1 Corinthians 10:1-11). We must press on continually, no matter how difficult the battle.

This is not as easy as it sounds. When God's plan is revealed, every devil tries to stop it. As Paul said:

Now thanks be unto God, which always causeth us to triumph in Christ.
2 Corinthians 2:14

After God's plan was revealed to us through Pastor Benny,

Beverly and I came under severe attacks of the enemy. Thankfully, He was dealing with us by removing layer upon layer of junk. We went through a purification process that I am sure is applied to every believer as he or she presses into the High Call of God.

I wanted to do something for God, and I had to start somewhere, so I began to volunteer every time there was something to do at the church. I will never forget the day one of the associate pastors called me into his office and told me he had something for me to do in ministry. I was elated. I just knew that God had ordained this meeting, and it was a divine appointment. I could already see myself as a prayer counselor, dressed in my Sunday best, ministering to God's people.

I was a bit puzzled when the associate began to talk to me about an upcoming pastors' luncheon. My first thought was that I was going straight to the top. I would be ministering to pastors. Boy, was I getting excited! Total confusion came over me when he told me to make sure to wear old blue jeans and tennis shoes. That did not seem to be in sync with the vision I had of myself, in my best suit, praying for the pastors.

Nevertheless, on the appointed day I arrived full of anticipation. I still wasn't sure what great things I would be doing for God, but it wasn't long before I found out. Someone handed me a pair of rubber gloves and told me to get busy.

After I became a pastor and shared this testimony, I told people I was the dishwasher that day. Beverly finally told me that I should stop promoting myself. In truth, my job had been to scrape all the uneaten food off the plates so that they could then be washed.

If that in itself wasn't humbling enough, the volunteer who really was the dishwasher kept sending word back to me that I wasn't getting the plates clean enough, and it was making her dishwater dirty. After about three hours of this, I finally got fed up. Under my breath I told the dishwasher to stick the plates up her nose, and I left. I wasn't quite sanctified yet and had only begun to understand the renewing of my mind.

As it turned out, the pastors' luncheon was a monthly affair, and I was invited to participate regularly after that. Although I didn't like the work at first, I kept going back to help, and invariably they gave me the same job each time I went. Each time I had to lay down my pride and humble myself before God, and I definitely began seeing a difference in myself.

Eighteen months went by, and from my perspective I was no closer to fulfilling God's call than before. During this time of wilderness waiting God was preparing me for the promise, for when it does come it comes suddenly. I have noticed that the Bible speaks about a lot of things being done *"suddenly."* In Acts 2:2, the Holy Ghost came *"suddenly."* In Acts 9:3, Paul was saved *"suddenly."* In Acts 16:26, he and Silas were delivered *"suddenly."*

God has said:

> *I have declared the former things from the beginning; and they went forth out of my mouth, and I showed them; I did them suddenly, and they came to pass.* Isaiah 48:3

> *Shall I bring to the birth, and not cause to bring forth?* Isaiah 66:9

What God has conceived in you He will cause to be birthed, and when it comes, it will come suddenly. All we have to do is press in and cling to His Word. We can use the knowledge of His plans He gives us through prophecy to fight the fight of faith and remain strong in the meantime. That is exactly what Paul told Timothy to do:

> *This charge I commit unto thee, son Timothy, according to the prophecies which went before on thee, that thou by them mightest war a good warfare.* 1 Timothy 1:18

God's Word is our strongest weapon during these wilderness times.

Beverly and I were not always strong, but by God's grace we continued to press in. One night I had a dream. I dreamed of the Second Coming of Christ. I was driving down a road, and around me buildings and trees were being consumed. People were rushing to get inside a huge cathedral or coliseum-type building. If they could just get into it, they would be safe. I woke up, and God said to me, "Preach My Word!"

By this time we had gotten back into the real estate business to support ourselves. We had another child and were enjoying serving the Lord as lay people. I had no idea where to begin a ministry, so I asked God: "How do I begin?"

He said to me, "See Benny."

I decided right then that God would have to open the door if I was going to see Pastor Benny Hinn. I told my wife and my mother about the dream and waited for further instruction.

To be honest, this frightened me terribly. I had told only two people about my call — my wife and my mother.

Three days later, at a volunteer picnic, Pastor Benny approached Beverly and me and said that three nights before (the same night and time I had the dream) God had spoken to him that I was to come on staff full-time as a pastor. I could not believe what I was hearing, and I quickly related my dream to Pastor Benny. That next night, in the evening service, I was placed into the office of Associate Pastor. It was August of 1988.

I was on my way to fulfilling God's purpose, climbing to the High Places. Pressing into the High Call of God in Christ Jesus had opened the door. The Scriptures remind us:

God is not a man, that he should lie; neither the son of man, that he should repent: hath he said, and shall he not do it? or hath he spoken, and shall he not make it good? Numbers 23:19

I had reached a new height in my spiritual experience, and my climb had begun in earnest.

Egypt was behind me, and the desert was ahead of me. There were only two choices: go back or push forward.

CHAPTER 6

PRESSURIZED FOR ALTITUDE

For my thoughts are not your thoughts, neither are your ways my ways, saith the LORD. For as the heavens are higher than the earth, so are my ways higher than your ways, and my thoughts [higher] than your thoughts.   Isaiah 55:8-9

Once again I am in flight. Today, as I prepare for takeoff on this Boeing 727, I am sharing my thoughts with you via this manuscript. Over the past ten years flying has become such a part of my life that I have related many spiritual experiences to the different processes of getting a plane off the ground and into the air. I wish I could take credit for the analogy that comes to mind today, but it isn't mine. However, it is a powerful truth that I pray will illuminate the way for those questioning any area of spiritual growth.

At six thousand feet, a plane must be pressurized. Although most of us don't pay nearly enough attention to the flight attendants when they go through their safety procedures checklist, we should, for they are giving us valuable, potentially lifesaving information.

One thing they tell us is that if the plane becomes depressurized, oxygen masks will automatically drop in front of us, and we will need to put them on and adjust them so that we can get the benefit of the oxygen.

The reason for pressurization is that the higher the plane goes, the greater the pressure exerted on it from the outside. The plane, therefore, must be pressurized from within so that it can resist the pressure from without. If the plane did not have the balance of this pressurization from within, it would implode.

This is exactly what the Lord does when He calls us to walk as disciples. We must be pressurized for altitude to walk in the High Places with Him. If we are not pressurized for flight, when we reach the High Places we will surely implode.

On our way to answering the High Call of God, we will be led by the Spirit into some intense times of pressure. During this time of training, our spirit man becomes so strong inside of us that no matter how much pressure comes from the outside, we are able to resist it and to maintain our climb. Just like the lifesaving information given to us on a natural airplane flight, this spiritual training will equip us for the pressures of life.

Speaking from experience, I have concluded that there are three main training camps which we, as believers, go through: (1) Wilderness Training, (2) Warfare Training and (3) Endurance Training. During my own pressurization training, I came to the understanding that our training never really ends. As we go from one level in our climb to the next, we must go through a similar process or preparation each time. Paul explained this perfectly in his letter to the Romans:

> *And not only so, but we glory in tribulations also; knowing that tribulation worketh patience; and patience, experience; and experience, hope.* Romans 5:3-4

How quickly we go through the training depends upon how quickly we can recover when the crosswinds of life try to blow us off the mountain. The Bible states:

Pressurized for Altitude

They [the Israelites] were overthrown in the wilderness.

1 Corinthians 10:5

Our first training camp is Camp Wilderness. Be well advised not to pitch your tents here. Keep moving forward. Our stay in Camp Wilderness is meant to be temporary.

The Israelites are a very good example of what not to do in the wilderness. Exodus 12 gives a detailed record of the Passover and of their incredible deliverance from four hundred years of slavery. In one night, the entire nation was freed.

They had prayed and believed for this day for many generations. From the time this generation had been small children, they had been taught of the covenant God had made with Father Abraham to make them a great and mighty nation. When Moses, their deliverer, finally came, he had already spent forty years in the wilderness himself.

Moses knew he had a destiny, but in his limited understanding he believed that by rescuing one Israelite he could fulfill the call on his life, and that his ministry would then "take off" (see Exodus 2:11-12). He was immediately taken into the desert, where God enlarged his capacity to understand what his true destiny was and the fact that it did not depend on his own strength, but on God alone.

Why did Moses have to experience this time of solitude in the wilderness? He would never have been able to take the people of Israel through the wilderness if he had not first experienced it himself. You cannot lead someone to or out of something you have not gone through yourself.

More importantly, it was in the wilderness that Moses' mentality was changed. He had started out with the faith to deliver a single Israelite, when God's plan was to use him to deliver the entire nation, numbering as many as two million, including men, women and children, *"in one night"* (Exodus 12:37). Be encouraged! Our wilderness experiences will work in us the capacity to accomplish God's plan for our lives. He wants to do above and beyond what we could ask or even imagine.

Paul wrote:

> *Now unto him that is able to do exceeding abundantly above all that we ask or think, according to the power that worketh in us.*
>
> Ephesians 3:20

God's desire is to equip us for the many challenges that await us, and He does it day by day while we are living the life He has given us.

When God spoke to Moses to go to Pharaoh and tell him to let the people go, Moses immediately began to make excuses, explaining to God why he wasn't the right man for the job. He had a whole list of excuses, and he started with the question: *"Who am I to go?"* (Exodus 3:11, my paraphrase). Although he saw himself as inadequate, this was a good question and the beginning of the turning point of Moses' life.

Moses' next question was: *"Who should I say sent me?"* (Exodus 3:13, my paraphrase).

God's response was, *"I AM hath sent you,"* (Verse 14, my paraphrase).

Unbelievably, Moses persisted: *"They will not believe You have appeared to me!"* (Exodus 4:1, my paraphrase). The miracles God then demonstrated (see Exodus 4:1-9) were for the benefit of Moses, to prove to him that God was indeed with him.

After God had supernaturally shown Moses that He would take care of all the details, Moses still had one more excuse: *"I am not eloquent ... I am slow of speech"* (Exodus 4:10).

God took care of this final series of excuses by telling Moses, *"Now therefore go, and I will be with thy mouth, and teach thee what thou shalt say"* (Exodus 4:12).

Moses did go to Pharaoh, and the Israelites were freed, but not before Egypt was struck with all manner of plagues. The miracles that God performed to sovereignly protect the people of Israel were for their own benefit, to build their faith in Him. Once Moses and Aaron had declared all the words God had spoken to them and had displayed all the signs He had shown them, the people believed (see Exodus 5: 30-31).

The psalmist recalled that great day of deliverance from Egypt:

He brought them forth also with silver and gold [the wealth of the Egyptians]: and there was not one feeble person among their tribes.
Psalm 105:37

As the children of Israel continued their sojourn, God supernaturally provided for them at every turn. The Red Sea was parted for them just in time to save them from Pharaoh's pursuing armies. They walked across the sea on dry land, and every single one of their enemies perished trying to do the same (see Exodus 14:19-31). A cloud led them by day, and a fire appeared at night to protect them (see Exodus 13:21). God provided manna from Heaven to feed them (see Exodus 16:4). Water poured forth from a rock so that they could have plenty to drink (see Exodus 17:2-6). They were on their way to the Promised Land, and everything was looking good.

The deliverance of God's people from Egypt was a result of answered prayer. It was also a shadow, or type, of our personal relationship with God. In my own experience, I received great deliverance from darkness (Egypt). I went through the waters of baptism (the Red Sea). The wonderful Holy Spirit met me (God's supernatural sustenance and provision in the wilderness). Still, after all of these great experiences with God, I found myself, as did the children of Israel, in a wilderness. Egypt was behind me, and the desert was ahead of me. There were only two choices: go back or push forward.

When I was first saved, I could sense that Jesus was right there with me at all times. All I had to do was whisper His precious name. Then came the morning I whispered, "Jesus ... Jesus .... Jesus? Where are you?" and there was no answer. I went from the Garden of Eden to Camp Wilderness in a very short time. Just the day before I had been confident in my salvation. I knew who Christ was, and I knew who I was in Him. Then, just that quickly, I had gone from total confidence to not even knowing for sure that I was really saved.

My mind was numb, and I had no direction and nowhere to turn. I was unsure of my future. All I knew was that either I had to go back to Egypt or I had to begin to trust God completely as my Source. Welcome to Camp Wilderness!

At the time, of course, I didn't know I had been recruited for a wilderness experience. I just knew everything had changed, and I had to be ready to move on.

The Word is clear about why we must spend time in the wilderness:

> *And thou shalt remember all the way which the* LORD *thy God led thee these forty years in the wilderness, to humble thee, and to prove thee, to know what was in thine heart, whether thou wouldest keep his commandments, or no.* Deuteronomy 8:2

The Israelites were taken into the wilderness *"to prove"* what was in them. It was no secret to God what was in their hearts, and it is also no secret to Him what is in ours.

There was a second reason for their wilderness experience. God *"suffered [them] to hunger"* (Deuteronomy 8:3) so that He could prove to them He was El Shaddai, the All-Sufficient One. Testing time in the wilderness proves two things: what is in our hearts and the fact of God's faithfulness.

When the children of Israel embarked on their journey through the wilderness on the way to the Promised Land, God had not abandoned them in any way. The Bible shows us that they lacked for nothing during their time in the wilderness. They were fed manna every morning, and water flowed from the rock to quench their thirst. Miraculously, their clothes did not deteriorate and their shoes did not wear out (see Deuteronomy 8:2-4). Their only problem was they could not provide for themselves. They were forced to completely trust God — FOR EVERY-THING.

In my own case, I lost everything that symbolized success to me. In the space of three months, my entire life as I had known it disappeared. God has a wonderful way of getting our attention. This all had to happen to free me of pride and to thrust me upon the provision of God.

I was so full of pride, even after I was saved, that God had no choice but to take me to the wilderness. Before I was saved, I had been hired by a large real estate corporation and was running a seven-million-dollar project for them — even though I was the youngest project director in their history. I had worked hard to get where I was, and I was proud of that accomplishment. To be honest, I was prideful.

Prior to being on Pastor Benny's staff, I wasn't sure what direction I should take. I knew God had called me, but I still had to support my family. My father owned a miniature golf course and go-cart track. He gave me a job standing behind the counter selling tickets. While there is certainly nothing wrong with selling tickets at a miniature golf course, for me it represented a long step down the corporate ladder I had worked so hard to climb.

It hadn't mattered much at first. While I was still in the Garden of Eden, right after my salvation, I wasn't really paying much attention to my surroundings. Now, at Camp Wilderness, I started noticing. In fact, I started getting sensitive about the matter. I would ask myself, *How in the world did I end up sweating in one-hundred-degree heat selling miniature golf and go-cart tickets, when I could be living it up back in my executive suite?* Once that kind of question entered my mind, it was followed by all sorts of accusatory commentary.

In the Sinai Desert there is no life. Nothing can grow there because of the intense heat and cold. As the Israelites wandered in that desert environment, God had to sustain them because there was nothing they could do to sustain themselves.

Because of their murmuring (despite the fact that God was providing everything they needed), they had to spend forty years wandering in the desert. The trip, even by foot, should have taken not much more than eleven days (see Deuteronomy 1:2).

I learned early in my own wilderness training that I could not shorten it, but I surely could lengthen it by being disobedient! The secret is that God walks us through the same experience repeatedly until our recovery period meets His requirements. If there is an area of your life that you have had to deal with over and over and over again, you can know that God wants to do something about it.

Each of us must face wilderness times in our Christian walk, so they will surely come to you. Until you come to the understanding that He is your only Source, you will still think you can accomplish something on your own.

Jesus Himself — the Lord of lords, the Everlasting Father, the Prince of Peace — was taken by the Spirit of God into the wilderness to be tempted of the devil (see Matthew 4:1). Why? So that He could come out of the desert with the power of the Spirit. When you go into the wilderness, you have God. When you come out, God has you.

As I went into the wilderness, Psalm 42 took on a whole new meaning to me:

> *As the hart panteth after the water brooks, so panteth my soul after*
> *thee, O God.* Psalm 42:1

As I would sing about the deer panting for the water or read this scripture, I would picture an ideal setting with a beautiful buck or doe standing in a shady alcove, gently lapping at the cool, refreshing water. The beauty surrounding the scene was breathtaking. The reality of this passage, however, is a totally different picture.

I have come to believe that the animal mentioned in Psalm 42 is being hunted, and the reason he is panting for the waterbrook is so that he can jump into the river and cause his enemies to lose his scent. Those who are hunters will know that this is often the only way a hunted animal can escape. He has an inborn sense that if he can just make it to some body of water, he has a chance of making it upstream without further detection, and possibly of escaping to safety. I am not ashamed to tell you that during the next phase of my training — my warfare training — I began to feel like a hunted animal. I was still traveling through the wilderness when suddenly it seemed that every devil who wasn't busy somewhere else showed up at my house. I went through a very tortured period.

Perhaps worst of all, I was suddenly assailed by a host of irrational fears. When I was about to go out, I would write down my telephone number for fear that I would get lost and not find my way back and would forget the phone number. This was very unusual because before I got saved I wasn't afraid of anything. Now I seemed to be afraid of everything.

Demons tormented me from early in the morning until late at night. The moment I woke up in the morning I would hear a voice saying, "I'm going to kill you today!" It was a terrifying experience.

David knew what it was to be surrounded by enemies. King Saul and his army were pursuing him, and he was desperate to find refuge. Like the hart, he had to find a way to lose his enemy (see 1 Samuel 23: 6-29). He needed a fortress, a safe camp and a river. He knew that if he could just get to the River of God he would be safe.

I know just how David felt. The spirit of fear gripped me like a steel vise. Everything in my life seemed to be falling apart. This all added up to a lot of strain on our relationship.

As I began to learn about dealing with spiritual attacks, I tried to rebuke the spirits attacking me, but they wouldn't obey me. The more I learned about spiritual warfare, the more intense the attacks became. There were days when I literally would not get out of bed for fear THIS would be THE day the enemy would make good on his promise to kill me. It was a horrible way to live. I certainly wasn't walking in the High Places during this time — in any sense of the word.

Nevertheless, God had a purpose in it all. I was being pressurized for altitude. God has His own ways of getting our attention, and He knew me far better than I knew myself. He made sure I got to the place He wanted me to be. I had no choice but to run to the River of God. I was driven to seek it by the spirit of fear. Let me say clearly that this was not a healthy fear of God. It was a fear of what would happen if I didn't get into His presence.

I spent hours reading the Word of God, and once I was able to get into His presence, I had peace. Just as soon as I would come out of the room where I had sequestered myself, the whole process would start all over again.

I lived in such fear of dying that I actually had to remind myself to breathe. This may sound crazy to some, but I would start to think about getting enough air into my lungs, and before I knew what had happened, I would be hyperventilating, struggling to get air.

This battle went on for two long years, and during all that time I stayed in a room, locked in with God, for as many hours of the day as I possibly could. I was studying everything I could about victory over demonic attacks. I had come across a wonderful book on the subject written by the late Dr. Lester Sumrall. I was happy to find it because I was undergoing so many different spiritual attacks that I simply had to learn what I was up against.

Then, about ten one night, after I had settled in and begun reading Dr. Sumrall's book, something very strange began to happen. If it had happened during the day, it might not have been such a terrifying experience. But it didn't happen during the day. It happened at night.

Beverly and the children were already in bed, and everything was quiet when I started reading. Then, out of nowhere I heard something making a noise: "Psst! Psst!"

I called out to Beverly and asked her what she was *psst, psst-ing* about. She told me she wasn't *psst, psst-ing* about anything. So I went back to my reading.

A few minutes later, I heard it again. "Psst! Psst!"

I put the book down, walked into the bedroom and said, "Beverly, why are you making that *psst, psst* noise?"

She said, "Kent, I am not making any *psst, psst* noise. I'm sleeping!"

I said, "If you are making a *psst, psst* noise, please stop. You're starting to frighten me!"

She said, "I promise you I am not making a *psst, psst* noise! Now please let me sleep."

I went back into the den and started to read, and immediately I heard it again. "Psst! Psst!"

I jumped up, ran as fast as I could into our room, jumped into the bed and said, "Beverly, listen to me. There is something out there. Would you go check it out while I pray?"

As I was being pressurized by outside circumstances, God was doing an incredible work on me inside. Even though I didn't realize how deep a work was taking place, I knew I was being changed from the inside out. God was enlarging my capacity to fulfill the call of being His servant. He was revealing pride, lack of security, fear of man, fear of failure and many other fears I didn't even realize I had.

I had learned a great deal during the wilderness and warfare training. Now God was allowing me to go through the season of endurance. It was time to stand upon His promises and trust Him to see me through. At the time, I was already a pastor. I was supposed to be the priest of my household, a mighty man of God.

Just as God lifted His hedge of protection from around Job (see Job 1:11-12) and allowed him to be afflicted, I believe He allowed the enemy to pursue me — to drive me into His Presence. I was to fight these battles for a season, and they did make me hungry for God. Jesus said:

Blessed are they which do hunger and thirst after righteousness: for they shall be filled. Matthew 5:6

This is not speaking of someone who has already become a spiritual giant. This is someone who has failed time and time again. This is someone who has come to the realization that he has no righteousness of his own. That is why he is hungering and thirsting for God's righteousness. Although my experience in this area was very painful and difficult, I would not have changed one second of it. Because of the spiritual attacks, I simply had to spend time in God's presence. I could not exist without His presence.

I had made the choice to go on to the Promised Land, not back to Egypt, and once that choice was made, I was completely in God's hands. He gave me the right to choose; but after I chose, the rest was up to Him.

I am thankful for all the training I received during this period of my life. Although I believe God allowed devils to drive me to the River of God (out of necessity for my survival), the result was that my foundation was solidly laid, and something could then be built upon it.

When Jesus cast a legion of devils into a herd of swine rooting on the Galilean hillside, the swine immediately threw themselves into the sea and perished (see Matthew 8:31-34). I believe this is a shadow of the spiritual realm. Devils cannot swim in the River of God. Just like the swine in this biblical story, they drown. So, if the enemy has been attacking your life, run with all your might to the River of God, where you can be safe.

There can be no doubt that such a river exists:

There is a river, the streams whereof shall make glad the city of God, the holy place of the tabernacles of the most High. Psalm 46:4

On our way to the High Places, God allows us to come to the end of ourselves. He reveals the motives of our hearts and what we are really all about. He has known all along, but for us to be of real service to Him, we must discover how very lacking in our own abilities we truly are. Paul wrote:

> *And base things of the world, and things which are despised, hath God chosen, yea, and things which are not, to bring to nought things that are: that no flesh should glory in his presence.*
>
> 1 Corinthians 1:28-29

> *It is no longer I who live, but Christ lives in me.*
>
> Galatians 2:20 , NKJ

When we come to the end of ourselves, we learn that we can never take credit for our own victories. We can never say that we have overcome. We must say:

> *I can do all things through Christ who strengthens me.*
>
> Philippians 4:13, NKJ

> *We are more than conquerors through Him who loved us.*
>
> Romans 8:37, NKJ

During the wilderness experience, we learn to use our weapons of spiritual warfare (see Ephesians 6:1-11), and as we learn to trust God to fight the battles for us by His Spirit, we move into the third training camp. We learn to wait on God and to endure and deal with our failures.

I can say very sincerely that it is through the failures of life that I have learned the most, not through my successes. This was true of the disciples as well. One of the greatest tragedy-to-triumph testimonies of all times is the story of the man called Peter, a fisherman turned disciple.

By all accounts, Peter was a rough Galilean who spent his days fishing on the Sea of Galilee. When Jesus called this crude man to spiritual service, he left his nets and immediately committed himself to the ministry. Although Peter had a rough exterior, he must have had a heart after God, for he remained with Jesus through thick and thin:

- Peter walked on water to get to Jesus (Matthew 14:28-29).
- Peter was with Jesus on the Mount of Transfiguration (Matthew 17:1-4).
- Peter was given, by the Spirit, the revelation that Jesus was the Son of God (Matthew 16:16-17).

As Peter and the other disciples were sent out, they saw people healed and delivered from sickness, infirmities, disease and evil spirits. Their mission was:

Heal the sick, cleanse the lepers, raise the dead, cast out devils: freely ye have received, freely give. Matthew 10:8

What a ministry! Peter probably felt as though he were walking in the High Places for sure, and he was. Still, God had an even bigger plan for this man's life.

Before Peter could fulfill the High Call, he had a few things to learn about himself. Just as an airplane has to be pressurized inside and out so that it will not implode, Peter had to become pressurized for altitude.

During his time with Jesus, he had always been outspoken. Right after his great revelation experience (recorded in Matthew 16:16), he put his foot in his mouth, when he began to rebuke Jesus as He warned the disciples that He would be killed by the elders, chief priests and scribes (see Matthew 16:22). Jesus knew what His own future held, and He also knew that we had no future if He failed to fulfill His destiny. His words to Peter, therefore, were strong:

> *Get thee behind me, Satan: thou art an offence unto me: for thou savourest not the things that be of God, but those that be of men.*
>
> Matthew 16:23

One might think that Peter would have learned to count to ten or to bite his tongue to keep his thoughts to himself after that scorching rebuke. Instead, the fire got a lot hotter for him.

God's refining furnace seems to be just about the same temperature as the refiner's fire in the purification process of gold. In our time the heat is measured much more scientifically, but in days past the only way to purify gold was to keep increasing the heat and drawing the dross off manually. This process was repeated over and over until the refiner had removed all of the impurities in the precious metal and he could see his own reflection in the pure gold.

God's hand was on Peter because He knew the destiny He had planned for Peter's life. God was pulling all of the dross out of him. He wanted to see His reflection in Peter.

Jesus warned Peter of the trial ahead:

> *And the Lord said, Simon, Simon, behold, Satan hath desired to have you, that he may sift you as wheat: but I have prayed for thee, that thy faith fail not: and when thou art converted, strengthen thy brethren.*
>
> Luke 22:31-32

It is notable that Jesus did not call His disciple Peter, the rock, on this occasion. He instead called him by his given name. That represented his old nature, one that he would very shortly revert to.

Again Jesus warned Peter, as He did the other disciples:

Watch and pray, that ye enter not into temptation: the spirit indeed is willing, but the flesh is weak.   Matthew 26:41

If he had heeded this warning, Peter might not have given in to fear when he was questioned about being part of Jesus' ministry (see verses 69-70).

Simon the fisherman, descendant of Jacob, could not in his own strength have made any changes in what was about to happen to him — even if he had wanted to. However, if Peter, the rock, had been obedient to pray, as Jesus had instructed him to do, he may not have had to endure the anguish of betraying the Lord whom he knew by revelation was *"the Son of the Living God."* Because Peter kept giving in to his flesh nature, he had to submit to the pressurization and the purification process over and over until he was completely emptied of himself, and only then could he fulfill his destiny.

Jesus spoke to His disciples just before He was arrested, and His words, again, were strong ones:

All ye shall be offended because of me this night: for it is written, I will smite the shepherd, and the sheep of the flock shall be scattered abroad.
                    Matthew 26:31

Peter, of course, jumped right in with his rebuttal:

Though all men shall be offended because of thee, yet will I never be offended.   Verse 33

Looking back, we can see what was coming, but Peter still hadn't learned all he needed to know and was blinded to what would follow:

Jesus said unto him, Verily I say unto thee, that this night, before the cock crow, thou shalt deny me thrice.   Matthew 26:34

Once again, Peter was right there with a quick answer:

*Peter said unto him, Though I should die with thee, yet will I not deny
thee.* Matthew 26:35

As we know, Peter denied the Lord he loved so much (see
verses 57-75). He denied Him once, then he denied Him again.
The third time, not only did he deny Christ, but he also cursed
Him (see verse 74).

That third time Jesus turned and looked Peter right in the eyes,
and immediately the cock crowed. Peter, realizing what he had
done, went out and wept bitterly (see Luke 22:61-62). There is no
way to know what Peter was thinking or feeling during the hours
after he denied his Lord. We can only imagine the depths of his
pain and remorse, from our own experiences with failure. We do
know, however, what was on Jesus' mind. He sent an angel to deliver a very specific invitation:

*Go your way, tell his disciples AND PETER that he goeth before you
into Galilee: there shall ye see him, as he said unto you.* Mark 16:7

Jesus knew the depths of Peter's anguish and knew that the
disciple would feel separated from his Lord because of his actions. His clear invitation proved that Peter was to not be left out.

After His resurrection, Jesus showed Himself to His disciples
three times over a period of forty days. During the third visit He
questioned Peter's love for Him three times. Each time, after Peter had responded and affirmed his love, Jesus told him (the
same man who had denied Him three times) to feed His sheep
(see John 21:15-19). Jesus was making sure that Peter was firmly
established in the ministry before He ascended to His heavenly
Father. The same Peter who had failed His Lord so miserably

was about to become one of the mightiest men of God in the annals of history.

On the Day of Pentecost, the Holy Spirit filled the disciples and changed their lives forever (see Acts 2:1-4). They all gave utterance to new tongues, but there was one among them who stood and boldly proclaimed the Gospel of Jesus Christ with great power. He was the same man who, just a few weeks before, had not only denied that he knew Jesus, but had also cursed Him. On that glorious Pentecost day, three thousand souls were added to the church, and from then on, Peter preached the Gospel wherever he went and multitudes were *"added to the church daily"* (Acts 2:47). Before long, the Spirit of God was so mighty upon Peter that his very shadow was known to heal the sick as it passed over them (see Acts 5:15). Peter had many failures, but he pressed on and became an example for all mankind to trust God to complete the good work He has begun (see Philippians 1:6).

The pressures of life will come. Situations will arise that can take us in exactly the opposite direction than we want to go in — if we let them. Sometimes the battles we have been fighting may seem to have no end. The wilderness, filled with warfare, failures and waiting, may seem to be an ongoing struggle. If this describes where you are, remember that you don't have to live forever in times of testing. You are just passing through. God will bring you out:

> *Thou hast caused men to ride over our heads; we went through fire and through water: but thou broughtest us out into a wealthy place.*
>
> Psalm 66:12

There is a popular print known throughout the world as "Footprints." The story tells of a man's walk with Jesus. At first there are two sets of footprints, then one. The man questions Jesus about His promise to never leave him, so why is there eventually only one set of footprints? Jesus responds by explaining that He carried the man through times of trial.

Recently, a new set of thousands of footprints has been added to this print. In this rendition of the story the man once again questions his Lord. He tells Him he understands that the two sets of footprints represent the two of them walking side by side, then the one set represents Jesus carrying him through trials, but what are all the thousands of footprints? Jesus answers and says, "That's where we danced when we made it through to the other side."

You are just passing through and, with Jesus carrying you and your trial, you will make it to the other side.

While you are being pressurized for altitude, God is drawing you closer to Himself. As you go through different danger zones, trust Him to get you safely to your destination, the High Places. Only He can do it for you.

If you will help other people achieve their dreams, goals and visions, in return, you will achieve yours. If you will continually seek ways to serve others and exalt them above yourself and your plans, then God will exalt you.

CHAPTER 7

SERVANTHOOD: GOD'S FORMULA FOR PROMOTION

But he that is greatest among you shall be your servant. And whosoever shall exalt himself shall be abased; and he that shall humble himself shall be exalted.   Matthew 23:11-12

With these words Jesus declared to us God's formula for exaltation or promotion.

From time immemorial the question has been asked, "How do I become great?" Millions of dollars are spent each year on programs, literature, training, conferences and seminars to learn how to become great. Even in the Kingdom of God there are growth conferences, seminars and training to make one successful in the Kingdom. No matter what direction you take in life — whether it is business, homemaking, being an employer, or being an employee — the way to become great or to succeed and rise to the top is to have a servant's heart.

A great motivational speaker once said, "If you will help other people achieve their dreams, goals and visions, in return, you will achieve yours." Another way of putting it is the scriptural principle: *you reap what you sow.* The Golden Rule, as we all know, is *"Do unto others as you would have them do unto you!"* If you will continually seek ways to serve others and exalt them above your-self and your plans, then God will exalt you.

Peter wrote in his first letter to the churches:

> *Likewise, ye younger, submit yourselves unto the elder. Yea, all of you be subject one to another, and be clothed with humility: for God resisteth the proud, and giveth grace to the humble. Humble yourselves therefore under the mighty hand of God, that he may exalt you in due time.*
>
> 1 Peter 5:5-6

When we exalt ourselves and place our desires above others, we are actually fighting against God. His Word is very clear that He *"resists the proud, but gives grace to the humble."* The grace of God will take us further and higher than we could ever take our-selves. The psalmist showed us that promotion comes not from the east or the west, but from God Himself (see Psalm 75:6).

I am reminded of a story of a man who came to a church desir-ing prayer that he might obtain a good-paying job. He explained that all of the positions he had applied for were filled. The pastor felt led to tell him to go back to a particular restaurant and tell the owner he would work for no pay. The young man was very sur-prised by this counsel, but since he seemingly had no other options, he did as he had been told.

The owner of the restaurant was just as surprised as the young man had been, but he allowed him to work anyway. After he had worked for a week, the owner was so impressed by his diligence that he not only hired the young man, but also, within a very short time, promoted him to the position of assistant manager. Why did all this happen? Because this young man humbled him-self, and God brought promotion to him.

Between the time I received the call to the ministry and the time God opened the door for me to actually be in the ministry, I was zealous to do something for God — anything. I knew what the Scriptures declare:

For we are his workmanship, created in Christ Jesus unto good works, which God hath before ordained that we should walk in them.

Ephesians 2:10

I knew I was supposed to be doing something in God's Kingdom. I just didn't know what that something was. Every time a ministry opportunity opened up, I was sure that was the position God had for me. Each time I tried to walk through a certain door, however, it closed. After a while, I was beginning to think maybe I was not really called at all.

In times of frustration such as these, we, as believers, must take a strong stand and hold on to what the Word of God has told us. When Jesus becomes our Lord, we accept the Great Commission to go and make disciples (see Matthew 28:18-20) and to do good works (see Ephesians 2:10). It is here that many believers lose sight of what the ultimate goal of servanthood really is. One all too familiar mistake believers make is trying to serve God in their own strength, not by the power of the Holy Spirit. When we do this, we easily grow frustrated wondering if God is ever going to use us.

Sometimes the frustration we feel is due in part to our own halfhearted commitment to serve. Other times it is because we simply are not aware of the real call of God on our lives. Because of these frustrations, such times of preparation and growth are often very difficult. Our frustrations become a weapon the enemy uses against us to discourage even those with the purest of hearts.

Being a servant requires giving our Lord the highest place in our lives. In the quest for finding our niche, we sometimes lose sight of the fact that it is He whom we are serving, and that the works we might do are secondary to that allegiance.

As I have said, God has His own ways of humbling us. I had been very successful in the business world, and then I was selling go-cart tickets at an amusement park. My whole mentality had always been to be a winner, and I knew I had succeeded in the world. Now, however, I was desperate to be promoted in God's Kingdom.

As I mentioned in Chapter 5, the one door that did open for me was volunteering at the monthly pastors' luncheon sponsored by our church. I wasn't prepared for the humbling experience of cleaning plates. I wanted to serve, but on my own terms, within my own comfort zone. I was waiting for my burning bush to speak to me or a lightning bolt to split the sky and knock me off of the pew. Like many who expect God to direct them in that way, I was disappointed. My direction came in the form of rubber gloves and a trash can.

I am confident that right now the Holy Spirit of God and the Word of God are leading and guiding you through circumstances and experiences that are preparing you and directing you right to the place you need to be to fulfill the call of God on your life. Believe it, and start looking for God's intervention in your life.

Dressed in blue jeans, sweat shirt and tennis shoes, scraping old food off of pastors' plates was definitely not my comfort zone. However, an amazing thing happened to me during this time in my life. I continued to serve at those monthly luncheons, and I began to enjoy my new job. It actually became fun. This was God's way of providing me the encouragement I needed to stay on course.

Jesus said:

Ye shall be sorrowful, but your sorrow shall be turned into joy.
John 16:20

We must keep our focus on the One we are serving, not on the particular work we are doing for Him at the moment. Little did I know that God was preparing me for the greatest adventure of my life, and, while doing so, He was creating in me a servant's heart. I began to experience great joy in serving others, and this is the key to successful ministry — service to God and man.

The revelation that I was serving Him — the King Himself — by serving others changed my life. The Word of God illuminates this truth brilliantly. Jesus Himself said:

Inasmuch as ye have done it unto one of the least of these my brethren, ye have done it unto me.   Matthew 25:40

To fulfill what God had called me to do, I needed a complete change of heart. For my entire adult life I had thought only of my own needs. God had much work to do in me. Serving in the ministry of helps was the beginning of my transformation.

I have already detailed how God spoke into my life through Pastor Benny Hinn and called me to work with him. In August of 1988, I became an associate pastor with a congregation of two hundred and fifty single adults under my pastoral care. The door was finally opened for me to preach, teach, pray, counsel, minister to and love this flock God had entrusted to me. It was, at the same time, exciting, frightening, demanding and rewarding. I loved everything about pastoring.

It was a great honor to work in that church, side by side with men and women who had been in the Kingdom for years. The church was experiencing phenomenal growth, and there was always something exciting going on. It was an absolutely incredible environment to be a part of.

As I became more comfortable in the position of pastor, I saw my dream, what I believed God had called me to do, being fulfilled. For three years I served the single adults at Orlando Christian Center, fully expecting to be with them for many years to come. God, however, had other plans. Very shortly another step in His plans would begin to unfold, and my life would suddenly take an entirely unexpected turn.

God has promised that if we will be faithful with that which is another's, He will cause us to have our own (see Luke 16:12). In 1990, Pastor Benny formed Benny Hinn Media Ministries. He had a dream and a vision to fulfill. While he was ministering in Singapore, God had spoken to him to begin miracle crusades throughout America. At the same time, he was also instructed to begin a daily national television broadcast. Through television he would be able to pray for thousands of sick, hurting people every single day.

While I was attending an area pastors' luncheon (this time as a minister, not a dish scraper), I heard Pastor Benny share this vision. While he was speaking, God spoke to my heart, "You will help him fulfill what I have spoken to him." A week later I was called into Pastor Benny's office for a meeting.

After a few minutes of small talk, Pastor began to tell me the reason for our meeting. Before he got very far, I politely interrupted him and said, "God has already told me that I will help you and serve you in this vision."

He asked me, "How do you know that?"

I told him how God had spoken to me during the luncheon, and he got very excited. It was, he said, the exact same time that God had spoken to him. That day I laid down my vision for the vision of another, but little did I know what great adventures lay ahead. For the next seven years I traveled the entire globe, serving Pastor Benny personally and ministerially. It was more fulfilling and rewarding than anything I had ever done in my life. I took care of arrangements for his meetings. I arranged transportation, checked the team into and out of hotels, ordered food, scheduled the itinerary, and even carried baggage. Whatever it took to insure that Pastor Benny was ready to minister, that's what I did. Aside from the heavy travel schedule and all it entailed, there was product development, ministering, counseling, miracle follow-up and building the staff.

I had many physical responsibilities as Pastor's personal assistant, but I also had the great privilege of being his traveling prayer partner. As the national crusades exploded all across America and the international crusades began all over the world, I was involved in every aspect of that ministry. God moved on our behalf, and many prayers were supernaturally answered.

There was no limit to my responsibilities. Whatever area of ministry needed to be taken care of, I learned to function in that capacity. My natural ability would never have sustained me during this time. It was only through diligently seeking the Lord's counsel and His wisdom (and having gone through my wilderness training) that I was able to do what was needed.

With the beginning of the crusades across America, *This Is Your Day*, Pastor Benny's daily television broadcast, hit the airwaves. I knew NOTHING about television, but, once again, I refused to lean on my own understanding and allowed God to stretch me and train me. The technology of the television media excited me, and for the first time I realized what wonderful capabilities were now available to preach the Gospel for Jesus Christ around the world to millions of people we might not otherwise reach.

When Pastor Hinn's partners' conferences were initiated, I, along with a dedicated staff, worked literally around-the-clock to make sure every detail was handled with a spirit of excellence. The experience and the training I received as part of that outreach were nothing short of miraculous and life-changing.

There were many others who served Pastor Benny at this time, but God supernaturally knit our hearts together and gave me favor in the area of knowing how to meet the needs of the man of God without having to be told what that need was. With the heavy travel schedule that he was maintaining, there were many special situations and daily issues that had to be resolved. Again, God gave me the grace to accomplish what needed to be done while I served in that great ministry.

Without the Holy Spirit I could never have fulfilled, in my own strength, what God had called me to do. With the call came the desire and the abilities to answer. This is one of the most amazing aspects of servanthood. Not only does God call us into ministry, but He also equips us for what He has called us to do. The only requirement is that we let go of pride, competitiveness, jealousies and whatever else gets in the way of our relationship with Him and get on with the Father's business.

The most amazing thing about what God did during the years I worked with Pastor Benny in his worldwide crusades was that I was still being prepared, trained and equipped. I had only known the Lord for a few years. What sustained me was that I had received the revelation that serving others meant that I was serving my God and King.

I would not want to give the impression that I always got things right — not in any sense of the word. I made many mistakes along the way, but the Holy Spirit was always right there beside me, leading and guiding me to my destiny.

Just as happens to all of us, there will be times in your life when you will feel put upon, used and unrecognized. When it happens, you must remember the promise of God that our labor is never in vain. There is a reward for those who serve.

Once I was flying home from an overseas trip. I had stayed behind to take care of some lingering details and to preach a church service, and I had to fly home alone. I was feeling a little sorry for myself when suddenly the Holy Spirit prompted me to read a passage of scripture that would impact my life for all eternity:

> *Fulfil ye my joy, that ye be like-minded, having the same love, being of one accord, of one mind. Let nothing be done through strife or vainglory; but in lowliness of mind let each esteem other better than themselves. Look not every man on his own things, but every man also on the things of others. Let this mind be in you, which was also in Christ Jesus: who, being in the form of God, thought it not robbery to be equal with God: but made himself of no reputation, and took upon him the form of a servant, and was made in the likeness of men: and being found in fashion as a man, he humbled himself, and became obedient unto death, even the death of the cross. WHEREFORE GOD ALSO HATH HIGHLY EXALTED HIM, and given him a name which is above every name: that at the name of Jesus every knee should bow, of things in heaven, and things in earth, and things under the earth.*
>
> Philippians 2:2-10

As I read, the Holy Spirit gently but firmly rebuked me. If Jesus, the very Son of God and equal with God, could lay aside everything to become a servant, how dare I feel discouraged because of my service? Many things in this passage spoke to me:

Verse 4 showed me that we are to look on others before ourselves.

Verse 5 showed me that we are to have the same mind as Christ about serving.

Verse 6 said, *"Who, being in the form of God, thought it not robbery to be equal with God."* Jesus laid aside His divine form, stripping Himself of divine glory and taking on the form of flesh, so that you and I — who are flesh — could be clothed with His glory.

Verse 7 said that Jesus *"made himself of no reputation."* He who holds the highest place of reputation in the universe, *"made himself of no reputation"* so that you and I can now be seated with Him *"in the heavenly places, far above all principality and power"* (Ephesians 1:20-21). Verse 7 also declares that Jesus took upon Himself *"the form of a servant."* We're talking about Jesus, the King of kings. He became a servant so that you and I — who are also called to be servants — could become kings and priests unto our God. The verse continues: *"He was made in the likeness of men."* Imagine! Jesus, the Son of God, became the Son of Man so that you and I — sons of men — could become sons of God.

Verse 8 says Jesus was *"found in fashion as a man."* Jesus allowed Himself to be tempted as man (yet without sin) so that you and I could now have a High Priest who can be *"touched with the feeling of our infirmities"* as men (Hebrews 4:5).

The verse continues: *"He humbled himself, and became obedient unto death."* Hebrews 2:14 declares *"... that through death he might destroy him that had the power of death, that is, the devil."* Jesus, by His death, destroyed death so that you and I — who were all of our lifetime subject to the bondage of the fear of death — might go free and have eternal life. Crucifixion was the most debasing and humiliating form of execution. What Jesus did on the cross for us was the lowest form of humiliation. Jesus, who knew no sin, became sin and died this most violent death, to pay the price for the sin of the world, so that you and I could be made *"the righteousness of God in him"* (2 Corinthians 5:21).

I wept as I thought of Jesus becoming a servant for me, and that day I vowed to serve Him in whatever capacity I could — forever. Being His servant is the greatest privilege in the world.

I had the honor of meeting the late Mother Teresa, one of God's wonderful servants and saints. This precious woman gave her life in service to hurting people. She told me, as she did everyone before she died, "Remember, when you do something for someone else ..." At this point she used her five fingers, as she held out her little, bony hand, her shoulders bent over from age and wear and tear on her body, and with a big smile, she said, "1. You 2. did 3. it 4. unto 5. Him!"

We must never forget — whether we are called to be a missionary, a businessman, a housewife or whenever we serve someone else out of a heart of love, as Jesus did for us — we are doing it unto Him. He said:

Inasmuch as ye have done it unto one of the least of these my brethren, ye have done it unto me.   Matthew 25:40

In the Kingdom of God, the way up ... is down. Servanthood is God's formula for promotion.

God is looking for people who will dare to go higher. If you insist on being average, you are as close to the bottom as you are to the top. God is calling us to go higher.

CHAPTER 8

LEAVING YOUR COMFORT ZONE

Eye has not seen, nor ear heard, nor have entered into the heart of man the things which God has prepared for those who love Him.

1 Corinthians 2:9, NKJ

It has been said that if you want something you have never had, you will have to do something you have never done. We all have what we now commonly call a "comfort zone." We are comfortable around certain people, surroundings, places, situations and assignments, but God wants to stretch us beyond our comfort zone to reach the High Places of fulfilling His will.

A way to determine if God is asking you to do something new and outside your comfort zone would be to ask yourself this question: Is it more than you can accomplish with the strength, resources, abilities and talents that you know you presently have? If so, God is calling you higher.

God has shown us that He wants to do *"exceedingly abundantly above all that we ask or think"* (Ephesians 3:20, NKJ). He wants you to do more, to soar higher, to experience greater things than you have ever dreamed of. His Word declares: *"Eye hath not seen, nor ear heard, neither have entered into the heart of man, the things which God hath prepared for them that love Him"* (1 Corinthians 2:9). When we leave our comfort zone, and only then, we will see the supernatural power of God. While living where we are comfortable, we have no need for greater power, greater strength, more of His gifts and provision. As soon as we step out beyond ourselves, we are met by God's help.

The Red Sea did not part until Moses stretched forth his rod. The Jordan River did not part until the priests stepped into the water. Peter would never have walked on water if he had not stepped out of the boat. Yes, he began to sink, but he knew what to do and called out to Jesus. On that occasion Peter prayed one of the most nonreligious and yet powerful prayers in the entire Bible, "Jesus, H...E...L...P!" Jesus did not despise this show of weakness on the part of Peter. He lifted Peter up, and they walked back to the boat together.

While I was praying recently, the Lord gave me an incredible revelation about walking on the water. In the Bible, water always represents the Word of God. When we step out of the boat (out of our comfort zone), we are taking a stand on the promises of God and trusting Him to make sure that we are on a solid foundation. As we continue our climb to the High Places, it is the written Word of God that sustains us, teaches us and encourages us. With each step toward intimacy with God through studying the Word, listening to the still, small voice of the Holy Spirit, and learning from our experiences, we are climbing higher and higher.

My friend Trevor Cockings put it this way:

"When I step out in faith, one way or the other I will find Jesus. Either my faith will produce and I will find Him as Jehovah-Jireh, my Provider, or I will begin to sink and cry for help and find Him as Savior. Either way, I'll find Him as I step out of my comfort zone."

There comes a time when God indicates to us in some way that

He wants to take us higher. The Holy Spirit puts a desire in our hearts to take the plunge or the leap of faith — no matter what the cost. We begin to desire to get out of the boat, even if we only walk on water for two minutes. We suddenly realize that it would be better to walk on the water for two minutes than to spend a lifetime in the boat. These are moments of opportunity, and we must respond to them. God is looking for people who will dare to go higher. If you insist on being average, you are as close to the bottom as you are to the top. God is calling us to go higher.

Throughout the Scriptures we find God asking men and women to leave their comfort zones and climb higher to fulfill their God-given destinies. In every case, it required faith in God's power, provision, protection and instruction to answer the call. Dare to step out of your comfort zone today and answer the call of God to fulfill your destiny in Him.

God called Abraham to leave the comfort of the modern city of Ur and take his family to look for *"a city ... whose builder and maker is God"* (Hebrews 11:10). God wanted to make Abraham the father of faith.

God called Joseph to leave the favored place he held at his father's side and to go into a pit and a prison and to go through much persecution, to eventually reach the palace in Egypt.

God called Moses to leave the comfort of being an Egyptian prince, to lead His people out of slavery and into the Promised Land.

God called Joshua to leave his place of service at Moses' side, to become the leader of all Israel.

God called David to leave the comfort of tending the sheep, to become king.

God called His beloved Son Jesus to leave the comforts of Heaven, to come to Earth and redeem all mankind.

111

Jesus, in turn, called disciples who left lucrative fishing businesses, government positions and more, to follow Him.

Today, the call of God is going out around the world for those who will come out of their comfort zones, take up their cross, and follow Christ.

In my own life, I had reached a very comfortable place serving Pastor Benny Hinn and his crusade team. I had been stretched by God to complete the assignment, and I had grown through the experience. I was able to travel all over the world, when I had never been out of the United States before. I was privileged to co-host the telecast *This Is Your Day* (obviously something I had never done before). I headed up a staff of the partner ministry department that recruited partners for the media ministry (something else I had never done before).

In each of these assignments I was being stretched and enlarged. I constantly had to believe God for the talent, strength and ability to perform each task. Because of my relationship with Him, I had now reached a comfortable place in the ministry. I felt secure in what God was doing in and through me.

My comfort was physical and financial as well as spiritual. My family was being well provided for, and I was so happy to be at Pastor Benny's side that I was ready to serve him in that capacity for the rest of my life — if that was God's will. I had reached a place of seniority in the organization, and I was content right where I was.

I was frequently reminded that God had placed a desire in my heart to preach, but I felt that I was fulfilling this part of my call by serving Pastor Benny as he preached and by occasionally preaching on my own. Then the word of the Lord came to me and everything changed. It happened in November of 1996 when I was in South Africa on a crusade mission with the ministry team. I awoke early in the morning and felt an urgency to pray. As I prayed, God spoke to me, "You are about to be launched out of this ministry. You will have My favor, and I will hasten My Word to perform it."

That night, while the team was preparing the auditorium for the night meeting, our sound man, Don Boss, came to me. He was trembling and tears were streaming down his face. He said, "I have never before had such an experience. God woke me up this morning and told me to tell you to pay the price and do what He was telling you to do." What a powerful confirmation of God's word that was for me!

Still, it was not easy to make the decision to leave Pastor Benny's side. Two months passed, and I had made no move. Then, suddenly, circumstances and situations began to push me toward making the decision to obey God. The Bible shows us that God is capable of speaking with a strong hand (see Psalm 89:13). The Lord spoke to me again, and this time He was far more specific. He said to me, "In the next ten years, you will travel the Earth preaching the Gospel. Your family will be by your side, and your strength will not fail you."

I was overwhelmed by this word, to say the least. What God was saying was far beyond my faith or my comfort level. I did not have enough faith to get from Orlando to Tampa to preach, much less to "travel the Earth." These are the times we sometimes question if we have truly heard from God. But God was also speaking through the circumstances of my life.

It reminds me of the way shepherds sometimes get their sheep moving. In the Eastern culture, there are still shepherds today. They are expert marksmen with rocks. When a sheep begins to stray away, the shepherd has the ability to fling a rock to hit just beside the sheep to steer it in the right direction. That is exactly what was happening to us.

Another analogy that has been used often for what God was doing is that of a mother eagle placing thorns in the nest of her eaglets so that they become so uncomfortable they will want to jump out of the nest. Although we were very comfortable in the natural, God was allowing us to become spiritually uncomfortable so that He could get us out of the nest.

I finally mustered up enough courage to approach Pastor Benny one day and share with him what was on my heart. I had long dreaded that moment, for several reasons. Not only had I become very comfortable with him and his staff, but he and many others in the ministry had become very comfortable with me. I would miss their fellowship and miss doing what I did for them. I had been in that place of ministry for nearly nine years, and I deeply loved the man of God and his team.

As I shared my heart, Pastor Benny surprised me. Rather than be upset that I had made this decision, he encouraged me. He told me, "I recognize God's call on your life and certainly do not want anything or anyone to hinder it." He told me that he often had to make such decisions himself as he pursued the High Call of God, so he understood how hard it was for me.

Graciously, Pastor Benny explained to me that he had been a traveling minister for many years prior to pastoring and beginning his crusade ministry. It had been a time of hard labor, with times of financial and physical struggle. He wanted me to be blessed in my endeavors, just as my own father would desire. He offered to continue to employ me as his assistant — with a full staff, salary and benefits — for two years. I would only have to work one weekend a month at one of his crusades, and the rest of my time could be spent traveling, fulfilling God's call. He also offered to contact his associates and other churches and suggest that they have me to minister for them. In this way, he would help me to build a ministry over time, until I was established and could go out on my own.

I could barely believe what I was hearing. This was too good to be true. It was like having your cake and eating it too. What a wonderful opportunity! As I prayed about this matter, God began to show me that He had very different plans. He wanted me to be totally dependent upon Him. He said to me, "It is time to leave Elijah and find the God of Elijah!" Although I was extremely grateful to Pastor Benny for his gracious offer, I knew what my decision must be.

My experience was not unique. Every servant of God experiences the moment when he must leave his Elijah (natural or spiritual fathers, those whom we have come to call mentors) and find the God of Elijah, the personal will of God for his own life. That doesn't mean our relationships with those who mentored us are severed. Quite the opposite is true. While serving others, we become disciples, and once we are trained, it is our responsibility to go and make other disciples and train them.

Based on what God had spoken to me, what I read in His Word, and godly counsel I had received from men and women of God whom I trusted, I made the decision to resign completely from Benny Hinn Ministries and to pursue the High Call of God on my own course. It was January of 1997, and I was taking a leap of faith into the unknown.

Beverly and I set up our first office in our home in Winter Park, Florida. It was furnished by two popcorn tins left over from Christmas. On one we placed the telephone, and on the other we placed an answering machine. Every morning we would get up, make a pot of coffee and go together into our new office. We would pray and then sit and wait for the phone to ring. After several days, it suddenly did.

Beverly and I both dived for the phone at the same time. The pastor on the other end of the line was not aware that my circumstances had changed and that I was on my own. We chatted for a while. Then after a few minutes he asked, "Do you preach?"

I said, "Yes, I do."

He asked, "Would you come to my church and preach?"

I replied, "Yes, I would."

He asked, "When can you come?"

I asked him to hold on while I checked my itinerary. I quickly told Beverly that I was accepting an invitation to preach, then came back on the line and said, "Tomorrow."

After that first call, our telephone has not stopped ringing. The Lord told me I would "travel the Earth," but I didn't realize I would do it in the first year of ministry. Nevertheless, in that first year on my own, I did literally circle the entire Earth preaching the Gospel. We preached all over the United States and from Europe to Australia to Africa.

I would be lying if I said all of this was easy. It was not and still is not easy, but oh, how rewarding it is to obey God!

The main reason many are unwilling to leave their comfort zones to go higher is fear. They are unsure that God will keep His promises. Jesus understood this fear and told a story (which is recorded in Matthew 25) about three stewards to whom talents were given. One of those stewards received ten talents, the second received five, and the third man received only one. The stewards who had received many gifts used their gifts well and were rewarded for doing so. The man who had received only one talent, however, was afraid. He said:

I was afraid, and went and hid thy talent in the earth.

Matthew 25:25

The result of this fear was tragic:

His lord answered and said unto him, Thou wicked and slothful servant.

Matthew 25:26

Fear had stolen from this steward the potential for fulfilling the call of God on his life. This is why the Apostle Paul exhorted Timothy:

Stir up the gift of God which is in you … . For God has not given us a spirit of fear, but of power and of love and of a sound mind.

2 Timothy 1:6-7, NKJ

Dr. Lester Sumrall used to say, "Feed your faith, and starve your doubts to death." Will Rogers once stated, "Hindsight is 20/20." When you look back to the past, you can see clearly the choices you could have made, should have made or would have made. But whatever you do, don't be bound by fear. Open your heart to faith. Step out of your comfort zone. Choose to follow Jesus — no matter what the cost. Fear will surely come knocking, but as a great man of God once said, "Fear knocked at my door. I allowed faith to answer, and no one was there!"

Don't live your whole lifetime in the boat. Kathryn Kuhlman, the well-known healing evangelist, used to say, "Many will be disappointed when they get to Heaven and find out how much they missed down here on Earth. Why ask for a cup, when there is a whole ocean available?"

The just shall not live by the anointing, the just shall live by faith. The anointing destroys the yoke of bondage, but it is by faith that we see it accomplished.

CHAPTER 9

ASCENDING UPON THE HIGH PLACES

Behold the proud, his soul is not upright in him; but the just shall live by his faith.　　　　　　　　　　　　　　　Habakkuk 2:4, NKJ

A man's pride shall bring him low: but honor shall uphold the humble in spirit.　　　　　　　　　　　　　　　　　Proverbs 29:23

For everyone who exalts himself will be humbled, and he who humbles himself will be exalted.　　　　　　　　　　　Luke 18:14, NKJ

As we ascend upon the High Places of God, at some point the pride of life will have to be addressed. You may ask, "Exactly what is the pride of life?" The pride of life is believing that you are invincible and nothing but good things will ever happen to you.

The pride of life wants to fulfill the lust of your eyes and flesh. It wants to succeed and prosper. It wants to do things in its own strength, without supernatural intervention from God. This is why our sin nature (the pride of life) has to be crucified and this is the reason Jesus died for us. When we allow our thoughts to become Jesus' thoughts and our will to become His will, He transforms us into His image and begins the process of preparing us for service.

As we study the Word of God, we see that man's failures are not always the danger, but rather his successes. It is often in the times of success and prosperity that we forget who our true Source is and begin to trust in our own ability to provide for ourselves. God is very diligent to warn us about that danger because even the spiritually mature can be enticed.

In 2 Chronicles we read of a man named Uzziah who became a king at the age of sixteen. We learn:

> *He did what was right in the sight of the Lord, according to all that his father Amaziah had done. HE SOUGHT GOD in the days of Zechariah, who had understanding in the visions of God; and as long as HE SOUGHT THE LORD, God made him prosper.*
>
> 2 Chronicles 26:4-5, NKJ

As long as Uzziah was seeking God as his Source, he was intellectual, famous and wealthy. God gave him many creative ideas, and he was known throughout the land for his inventiveness. However, something happened and Uzziah fell. The reason for his fall is clearly stated in the Scriptures:

> *But WHEN HE WAS STRONG his heart was lifted up, to his destruction.*
>
> 2 Chronicles 26:16, NKJ

Uzziah forgot God and began to trust his own strength. He began to allow the power that God had given him to puff him up. He started to believe that he was in control, forgetting that it was only as he sought God that he was exalted. Uzziah's story has a sad ending. He died a leper, cut off from the House of God.

When we study church and world history, we see many men falling, not when they were weak, but when they were strong. God warned Israel against the enemy of pride:

For the LORD your God is bringing you into a good land, a land of brooks of water, of fountains and springs, that flow out of valleys and hills; a land of wheat and barley, of vines and fig trees and pomegranates, a land of olive oil and honey; a land in which you will eat bread without scarcity, in which you will lack nothing; a land whose stones are iron and out of whose hills you can dig copper. When you have eaten and are full, then you shall bless the LORD your God for the good land which He has given you. Beware that you do not forget the LORD your God by not keeping His commandments, His judgments, and His statutes which I command you today, lest - when you have eaten and are full, and have built beautiful houses and dwell in them; and when your herds and your flocks multiply, and your silver and your gold are multiplied, and all that you have is multiplied; when your heart is lifted up, and you forget the LORD your God who brought you out of the land of Egypt, from the house of bondage; who led you through that great and terrible wilderness, in which were fiery serpents and scorpions and thirsty land where there was no water; who brought water for you out of the flinty rock; who fed you in the wilderness with manna, which your fathers did not know, that He might humble you and that He might test you, to do you good in the end; then you say in your heart, "My power and the might of my hand have gained me this wealth."

And you shall remember the LORD your God, for it is He who gives you power to get wealth, that He may establish His covenant which He swore to your fathers, as it is this day. Then it shall be, IF YOU BY ANY MEANS FORGET THE LORD YOUR GOD, AND FOLLOW OTHER GODS, AND SERVE THEM AND WORSHIP THEM, I TESTIFY AGAINST YOU THIS DAY THAT YOU SHALL SURELY PERISH."   Deuteronomy 8:7-19, NKJ

God gave warning to the people of Israel — after He had blessed them, prospered them and exalted them — to beware lest they forget Him, the One who had empowered them to receive promotion and honor. Once again we see the warning to beware of falling not in time of lack, hardship or trial, but in the time of peace, prosperity and power.

The Apostle Paul declared:

> *And lest I should be exalted above measure by the abundance of the revelations, a thorn in the flesh was given to me, a messenger of Satan to buffet me, lest I be exalted above measure.*
>
> 2 Corinthians 12:7, NKJ

According to Webster's New World Dictionary, pride is "an over high opinion of oneself; exaggerated self-esteem; conceit; the showing of this in behavior; haughtiness; arrogance." In the natural realm, this is a very accurate definition. However, there are many forms of pride that manifest when we are trying to get to the root of a spiritual issue.

Any time we are functioning in our own strength and not depending on God to provide in every area of our lives, an element of pride has entered in. Not only can pride enter into your life because you are prospering and successful; it can also come in the form of fear, insecurity, doubt and false humility. There are many different kinds of pride, and they all open the door for an onslaught of the enemy.

One of the areas that must be dealt with is the fear of man. This particular vulnerability is something we are all susceptible to. When we are more concerned about the acceptance of our peers than what God is saying and doing, pride has crept in through the fear of not being pleasing in the eyes of man.

No one wants to fail, but it becomes all the more difficult when you have an audience. In the natural realm, being humbled usually comes from the humiliation of failure. However, true humility comes from depending completely on the Creator:

God resists the proud, but gives grace to the humble. Therefore humble yourselves under the mighty hand of God, that He may exalt you in due time.   1 Peter 5:5-6, NKJ

Paul, who was called to the third heaven and given an abundance of revelation, said that he was, by the grace of God, given *"the messenger of Satan to buffet [him], lest [he] should be exalted above measure" (2 Corinthians 12:7)*. He realized that God's grace was what he would have to depend upon, not his own strength:

My grace is sufficient for you, for My strength is made perfect in weakness.   2 Corinthians 12:9, NKJ

If it is our heart's desire to walk with God in the High Places, we must be willing to allow Him to send messengers, whether they come in the form of trials, circumstances, demonic forces or the enemy himself, to buffet us. During these times we must know that it is His grace that sustains us. When we truly desire to serve Him and know Him more intimately, there comes a time of sifting that removes the silt from our lives and releases the authority we are called to walk in as believers.

We begin to partake of the suffering that Jesus endured on the cross, the suffering that set us free and enables us to walk with Him. Because we cannot see Him, it is a walk of faith. As we continue to climb God's holy mountain, it takes faith to complete the climb.

After being released into ministry, Beverly and I experienced great blessings in the first year and a half that we traveled. Supernaturally, the Lord opened doors around the world for us to minister and preach the Gospel. God had promised us that we would travel the Earth preaching His Word, and in the first year that is exactly what happened. We literally circled the whole globe. We preached in Europe, England, Australia, Indonesia, Argentina, Africa, the Netherlands Antilles and all over the United States.

God's provision was abundant. We saw many people blessed and touched by the anointing of the Holy Spirit. The gifts of the Spirit were being poured out through our lives. The word of knowledge was incredibly accurate, and many people were born again and healed by the power of the cross.

There was such joy in our lives. Everything we touched seemed to prosper. It was thrilling to be used of God in this way. There is really nothing that compares to the exhilaration of knowing that the Most High God is working through you to touch His people.

It was so exciting experiencing God's fulfillment of His promises to us. Financially, we were living totally by faith, and miraculously funds flowed into our ministry, not only meeting our needs, but also allowing us to give to others liberally.

I traveled to Argentina in August of that year to minister, and while praying in my hotel room, God spoke these words to me, which I recorded:

> *Dare to climb My Holy Mountain. Dare to tread upon My High Places where few have trod. Climb as Moses did to receive commands. Climb as My Son Jesus did to be transfigured. Climb in faith to reach the High Place, so that you will suck honey out of the rock, and your steps will be washed with butter, so that every place you step, My anointing will flow freely.*

His voice and direction for me was so clear that I did not doubt that I was hearing the Lord's plan for the future.

In the ensuing weeks there were many powerful manifestations of the Holy Spirit happening each time I shared the Word of God, so much so that I began to think, "What a quick trip to the top of the mountain!"

I knew God had called me to go even higher, but I didn't understand that to get there I would have to face old foes that I believed had long since been vanquished. God wanted to reveal to me through facing these old enemies that the mantle of anointing on my life had little to do with my personal relationship with Him.

The gifts and calling of God are without repentance. History has shown us that there have been men and women ministering powerfully under the anointing of God, while personally they were living defeated lives in their walk with Christ.

It is imperative that as believers we judge a ministry by its fruit and not by its gifts. According to the Gospel of Matthew we are to judge a tree by its fruit (see Matthew 12:33). We must take the long-term view, as God does, and remain longsuffering in our love for those who are struggling to keep a just balance between the gifts of the Spirit and the fruit of the Spirit. It is indeed rare to come into contact with an individual who intentionally planned to fall short of accomplishing what God called him to do by falling into the pit of pride.

We need to make sure that we are being trained daily, by staying in close communion with our Heavenly Father. It is this intimacy that will protect us from allowing pride to overtake us when the gifts of the Spirit are in operation in our lives.

One of the greatest examples of this in the Bible is the story of Aaron and Miriam, Moses' brother and sister. Because they, too, were prophets, they took it upon themselves to point out to Moses that they also heard from God (see Numbers 12:1-16). The two of them rose up against Moses in rebellion, and Miriam was immediately struck with leprosy. She was banished from the camp for seven days and could not return until Moses had prayed for her to be healed.

Aaron, on the other hand, was not struck with leprosy. To his credit, he confessed their sin. However, his repentance is not what protected him. His priestly garment, which was symbolic of God's anointing on his life, is what protected him. As long as he was functioning in the capacity of his priestly anointing he was protected.

Even though God was longsuffering, there came the time when Aaron was stripped of his priestly garments (his anointing), and he died on top of Mount Hor in front of the very congregation he had led in rebellion (see Numbers 20:22-29). We will not be judged by what we have done with the anointing of God, rather we shall be judged according to whether we have robed ourselves with salvation and righteousness.

God showed me that if I would be concerned with righteousness and humility, I would never have to be concerned about the anointing. If I would take time to put on my robe of salvation and righteousness, He would take care of the robe of the anointing. In other words, if I would take care of my underwear, He would take care of my outerwear.

In pursuit of the High Call, I was enjoying all of God's blessings, and the gifts of the Spirit were operating in my life. However, without realizing it, I had succumbed to the temptation of serving God because of what He was doing, not because of who He is.

Proverbs shows us what keeps many people from totally trusting the Lord to accomplish His plans for their lives:

> *The fear of man brings a snare, but whoever trusts in the LORD shall be safe. Many seek the ruler's favor, but justice for man comes from the LORD.*   Proverbs 29:25-26

Fear of man and fear in general are based in pride. I was bound by fear and false humility, which both have their roots in pride. I had begun to trust my own abilities to minister and provide, rather than God's. It didn't happen out of blatant pride and haughtiness, but out of fear and insecurity.

These spiritual enemies take our trust away from God because we are looking to ourselves and not to Him. I thought I was at the top of the mountain, when I realized I hadn't even begun to climb. My real journey was about to begin.

Five years previously, I had been rushed to the emergency room in severe pain. I was diagnosed with gallstones and an inflamed gallbladder. Emergency surgery was recommended. While sitting in a darkened x-ray room, I prayed and God gave me a scripture. At the time, I did not realize this word from the Lord was a scripture, but I later found it in Jeremiah. It states:

> *"Is not My word like a fire?"* says the LORD, *"and like a hammer that breaks the rock in pieces?"*   Jeremiah 23:29, NKJ

I was taken aback by this word, but in faith I placed my hand on my stomach, quoted this scripture and was totally healed. For five years I had been free of all symptoms.

Shortly after the meeting in Argentina, where God had spoken to me so clearly, I headed to Reykjavík, Iceland. After five years of being completely pain free, the same pain had returned while I was ministering in Iceland. The first thing I did, of course, was to place my hands on my stomach and quote Jeremiah 23:29. I did it once, then twice, and finally three times, but I gained no relief.

Upon arrival back in Orlando, I was taken back to the hospital and again diagnosed with gallstones. After being healed of the first bout of gallstones, a sonogram had shown that they were gone. Now, they were back. I continued to confess the Word, but the pain did not leave, and once again the doctors suggested emergency surgery.

Beverly and I began to seek the Lord and His direction concerning the procedure. Should I have it, or should I trust Him to heal me, as He had before? The Lord was silent.

After Iceland, I was scheduled to preach in Germany and then go on to Africa. The doctors warned me strongly that I did not want to have this type of surgery in a third-world country if I could avoid it. The best choice would be to go ahead and take care of the problem at home. It was major surgery, but because of new medical technology it was considered to be a simple procedure.

I decided to go through with the operation, and within twelve hours I was less one gallbladder. Unfortunately, I had a severe reaction to the anesthesia, and this turned a simple procedure into a major ordeal.

Because the anesthesia had made me sick, I had to take an anti-nausea drug that I had an allergic reaction to. This set back my recovery, but the real torment began when the doctor came in and told me they may have missed a stone and would have to put an endotracheal tube into my mouth, down through my stomach and possibly probe my small intestine.

After several more tests, it was determined that the surgery had been a success after all and there would be no need for the tube to be inserted. I was sent home two days after the surgery to recuperate.

Beverly took me home on the morning of September 9th, but by six that evening I was back in the emergency room. My body was rebelling against the different medications I was taking, and my mind was overwhelmed by fear.

I spent three more days in the hospital and eventually received relief physically when they stopped the medication I was on. Physically I was "on the road to recovery," but emotionally the battle had just begun.

In the days ahead I came under severe attack from the enemy, in my mind. The same enemies that had tormented me in the early days of being in the ministry struck again with a vengeance. A terrible spirit of oppression and fear came against me. I would try to pray, and it felt as if a claw was ripping into my mind.

I was fearful of dying, tormented by the spirit of death, thinking my ministry was over, that I would not see my children grow up, that I would die a young man, not having fulfilled the call of God or seeing His promises fulfilled in me and through me. I quoted the Word, prayed and praised, anything and everything I knew to do. Still, the onslaught of darkness could not be broken. I became desperate to hear the voice of the Lord.

When Beverly and I had prayed for several days and there was no breakthrough, I called my friend Trevor. He has an incredible prophetic mantle on his life and has spoken truth into my life throughout our long friendship. I was searching for answers and began to pour my heart out to him.

Little did I know what the outcome of this conversation would be. Before I knew what had happened, Trevor had told me all of the problems he was having in his ministry, and instead of feeling better, within minutes I felt as though I had been dragged down to the bottom of the ocean and was being completely overwhelmed.

When he finally finished, I began to cry out that I was desperate for God. I realized I had been looking to man for an answer that only God Himself could give me. Trevor grew very quiet on the other end of the phone line, and we both began to sense the anointing of the Holy Spirit like I had never experienced it before. It seemed as though a river of God's presence began to flow over both of us. When I confessed out of my mouth that I was desperate for God, I realized for the first time what it really meant for His strength to *be made perfect in weakness.*

It was during this conversation that I had the first glimpse of where I was and what God was revealing to me. I had been looking everywhere, hoping someone could tell me what to do and how to break through the darkness I was in. I was so deep in it that I thought I could not get to Jesus.

I had read books, I had sought counsel from men, and I had gone to meetings, but what Jesus wanted was for me to be completely dependent on Him. My flesh nature was being crucified. What I had yet to realize was that I would not stay in this state. I had to go lower so that Jesus could take me higher.

I had become desperate for His presence in a way that I had never known before, and once I confessed that I was desperate for Him — even though I thought I could not get to Him, Jesus came to get me.

David had this same experience. He could not find God, so he asked God to please find him:

> *I have gone astray like a lost sheep; Seek Your servant.*
>
> Psalm 119:176, NKJ

There was the absolute knowledge that I could accomplish nothing without God. I had to be dependent on His strength because I had none of my own.

I had been begging God to speak to me, and He had been doing everything He could to get my attention. Now He had my undivided attention. I was listening.

At 5:30 a.m. on Wednesday, September 16, 1998, I awoke out of a deep sleep to the sound of my Savior's voice. Over the next few hours, He spoke so clearly that there was no doubt that what He was about to impart to me was of the utmost importance.

I saw the earth, and it was cracked and dry. I thought at first He was going to explain this vision and relate it to the natural water tables of the Earth. However, it seemed as though the Lord knew my understanding would be limited and that I would lack the knowledge to grasp what He was saying. Seemingly He was frustrated, knowing that I would struggle to understand the significance of what He wanted to tell me.

I know that what I am about to say may seem strange to some, but this is exactly how it happened and exactly what the Lord spoke into my spirit in the early morning light. He simply said, "Just listen. Get up and move. Your river of provision has dried up. I brought you to this place (Orlando, Florida). I healed you, blessed you, imparted to you and called you, but now it is time to move. I have prepared a place for you in Alabama and widows to sustain you."

Shockingly, God said, "I'm sorry I had to allow you to go through this, but I had to place a stone in My eagle's craw to set you down and keep you from flying so I could speak to you."

He said to me, "I have not allowed you to go through this to show you that you must go through things. I have allowed you to go through this to show you that if you will stay close to Me, through prayer and fellowship, I can speak to you and keep you from going through things! At this time it will be detrimental to you and to My Kingdom if you do not obey. Remember that when Israel lagged behind the cloud they were smitten by the Amalekites, so stay close to Me."

I realized that in my time-consuming travels I had gotten so busy trying to go higher that I had forgotten the One that I was climbing to see.

I was told later by a pastor who had grown up on a farm that eagles and chickens have no teeth and must ingest little stones in their craw or gizzard, which grinds up their food, so they can digest it. If they ingest too large a stone, it holds them down and they can't fly.

I wish I could tell you my trial ended right then, but it didn't. There was yet another important lesson for me to learn. Even though the Lord had spoken very clearly to me and I had sensed His presence in such a tangible way, there was an area that still had to be dealt with. I had to come to the place in my relationship with Him that I would no longer live by what I saw or felt. I would have to begin to live completely by faith and to trust God like I had never been able to before.

The week after I had been released from the hospital, I had to go through a series of tests for heart problems and was diagnosed with mitral valve prolapse. I don't know if the surgery and ensuing physical problems aggravated an undiagnosed condition, or if this new problem occurred as a result of the combination of the two. During the period shortly after the gallbladder surgery, I had suffered such a bad physical reaction to the medication I was given that instead of getting stronger I was growing weaker and weaker.

The spirit of fear attached itself to me, and with fear had come the spirit of death. I thought that I was literally in a battle for my life. My heart had started to beat irregularly, and in my weakened spiritual and physical state, I thought my time on this Earth was coming to an end.

My body had yet to recover from the surgery that had taken place on September 7th, and with the heaviness of this new diagnosis hanging over my head, I sank even lower into the darkness and oppression that was surrounding me. I spent the entire month of September in and out of heart specialists' offices, having every heart test administered that was available. We had to cancel all of our meetings for the month. Spiritually, emotionally, physically and financially, things were becoming very, very strained.

In the middle of this process of recovering from gallbladder surgery and the shocking discovery of the mitral valve problem, I traveled to Alabama in pursuit of the place God had told me to move. Even though I was weak physically, I believed that if I kept pressing into what God had spoken to me, the chains would be broken off of my mind, and I would be set free. I was overwhelmed by the darkness that I was facing on every side, but I knew that if I stopped I would be defeated.

In the days that followed, I literally lived each moment by faith. I was not always successful. I became even more desperate for God. I had to have Him and His help.

I was scheduled to start preaching again on October first. I was in my hotel room before the service and could not get out of bed. I was weak, fearful and anxious. Basically, I was overwhelmed and defeated.

In the sanctuary of the church where I was scheduled to preach that Sunday night there were more than nine hundred people waiting for my arrival. Little did they know that I was trapped by fear, still in my bed.

As I lay there that night, in tears, I told Beverly I could not go, I was finished, she needed to check me back into the hospital or into a sanatorium. I could not get up.

Beverly, who loves me faithfully, was very compassionate — at first. She consoled me and spoke quietly, comforting me as only she can do. That lasted for just about ten minutes. After expressing her deep love and concern for my condition, she began to speak slowly and deliberately. She looked at me with fire in her eyes and spoke these words, words that I will never forget as long as I live: "Kent, I am not going to let the devil steal from you any longer! I'll tell you what you are going to do. You are going to get up out of that bed, you are going to take a shower, and you are going to put a suit on. We are going to church, and you are going to preach tonight. If you die, you will die preaching."

Those were strong words, and I knew she was right, but I did not have the will to get up. She then shifted into battle mode and began to call our friends around the United States. With them, we began to pray, agree and take authority over the enemies that were fighting to keep me bound.

I did preach that night. I told those who had assembled at the church that I was just like them. I was desperate for a touch from God. With tears streaming down my face, I invited those who were also desperate for His presence to join me at the altar. Two hundred and thirty men, women and children came to the altar that night. I was still sick in mind and body, but by faith I trusted God, by His precious Holy Spirit, to accomplish what only He could do.

God can work through a broken, cracked vessel if that vessel will only yield to Him, and there is no doubt that I was broken before Him that night.

That was the beginning of a forty-five-day trip. Beverly literally held me by the hand and escorted me to the services. In those forty-five days I preached in Alabama, Georgia, England, Germany, Canada, Africa and North Carolina. I was numb.

During this time I felt as though God was a million miles away, but in reality He had never been closer to me. When I prayed, I didn't sense His presence. As I ministered to others and the power of God flowed, changing lives, I felt nothing. The fear and the physical problems escalated.

I knew I was called to preach, and I knew God had anointed me to fulfill that call, but the darkness surrounding me was beginning to take its toll. I began to question if I was even saved, much less called to see others won for Christ. I searched for answers through prayer, studying the Word of God, and reading literature written by others who had experienced similar issues.

It was during this time that the Lord showed me that the just shall not live by the anointing, the just shall live by faith. Yes, the anointing destroys the yoke of bondage, but it is by faith that we see it accomplished.

We must take the step of trusting God to fulfill what He has already promised us in His Word:

Now faith is the substance of things hoped for, the evidence of things not seen. Hebrews 11:1

I definitely had to trust God. In my own strength I couldn't even get out of the bed.

In the beginning of this trial God had told me to get up and move. Right after He spoke to me, we attended a miracle crusade in Birmingham, Alabama. The trip had been unplanned, but I was desperately seeking the river of God, so we went. Looking back, I realize now how much God was in that trip. It was just a short drive from Birmingham to the area where I believed God was directing me to move. My family lives in the neighboring town, so we called to enlist the aid of my sister, Ann.

At first she was skeptical that there would be a home in the area on the market large enough to accommodate our needs. After researching the real estate market, she found one property that she thought might work.

We drove directly to the town of Lineville, Alabama, after the crusade. Our appointment to see the property was not until the next day at 1:00 p.m., but there was already very tangible expectancy in our spirits about the prospect of moving to this beautiful countryside.

After viewing the property, we knew it was to be our new ministry headquarters. We agreed to buy it right then and there. Since we had no money for a down payment, we secured the deal with a handshake. This was the first confirmation that God was working behind the scenes.

Upon returning to Orlando we put our house on the market, and it sold in three weeks. We were in Canada when the first bid came in, and it sold while we were still on the road. The sense of expectancy again quickened in our spirits.

We began to realize that our heavenly Father was moving on our behalf, and the move was going to be exciting. Although we believed God had spoken to us, the sale of our home was the final confirmation.

Throughout all of our traveling, the sale of our home, and, ultimately, the move to Alabama, I still was not victorious. There were victories along the way, but I was in the middle of the war.

As we prepared to move, the knowledge that God was orchestrating everything was a great comfort, but I still had to battle every step of the way. On the first of November, Beverly and I went in separate directions. She went to prepare our new residence and office, and I left for Africa for ten days of outdoor crusades.

It was in Africa that I really came to the end of myself. The voodoo priests beat their drums for days trying to bring down rain so the meetings would be canceled. In the spiritual realm there was a great battle raging that would have been difficult to deal with under any circumstances. In my current state of mind, they were overwhelming. I had to stand on the reality that God had a plan and purpose for my life (see Jeremiah 29:11), I had to let go of the things in my life that I was unsure of and that I was afraid of, and I had to die to myself and let Jesus Christ live His life through me.

There comes a point in every believer's walk of faith that they literally die to their own fleshly desires. I had heard this taught for many years but never fully understood that there is a very real death. Kathryn Kuhlman, who was used mightily of God in the ministry of healing, shared publicly that she could take you to the spot where she died to self. I now have a better understanding of what that experience worked in her life.

Personally, this was the greatest test of faith I had ever dealt with. It was the turning point in my life that revealed my utter dependence upon my heavenly Father. It was the place of death to my flesh, my desires, and to anything that wasn't completely dependent upon Him.

Paul encouraged the Galatians with these words:

> *I have been crucified with Christ; it is no longer I who live, but Christ lives in me; and the life which I now live in the flesh I live by faith in the Son of God, who loved me and gave Himself for me.*
>
> Galatians 2:20, NKJ

God proved Himself faithful to sustain me, and I continued to trust in Him. I had no other choice. Faith really is *"the substance of things hoped for"* and *"the evidence of things not seen"* (Hebrews 11:1).

Paul revealed how faith triumphs over trials:

> *Therefore, HAVING BEEN JUSTIFIED BY FAITH, we have PEACE with God through our Lord Jesus Christ, through whom also we have access BY FAITH into this grace in which we stand, and rejoice IN HOPE OF THE GLORY OF GOD. And not only that, but we also GLORY IN TRIBULATIONS, knowing that TRIBULATION PRO-DUCES PERSEVERANCE; AND PERSEVERANCE, CHARAC-TER; AND CHARACTER, HOPE. Now HOPE DOES NOT DIS-APPOINT, because the love of God has been poured out in our hearts by the Holy Spirit who was given to us.* Romans 5:1-5, NKJ

These reminders about faith are invaluable to those who are struggling with different areas in their Christian walk.

1. By faith, we have been justified.
2. By faith, we have peace with God.
3. By faith, we have access to God.
4. By faith, we hope in the glory of God.
5. By faith, we glory in tribulations.
6. By faith, tribulation produces perseverance, perseverance, character and character, hope.
7. By faith, hope does not disappoint.

I did not come out of this battle in my own strength, but through diligently pressing into God. I had to depend on His grace, His mercy, His strength, His provision and His faithfulness to keep His covenant with me.

While resting in Alabama during the month of December of that year, I was fellowshipping with the Lord. He spoke very tenderly and told me that the whole time it had seemed as though I was spiraling downward, I had actually been climbing.

While praying and asking the Lord for direction, I heard His voice telling me that I would never see these enemies again. All the fears I had battled my entire life had been dealt with. There will be other battles to face, but I know, by faith, that I will never see these enemies again.

Although this had seemingly been a very dark time in my life, it had also been the most enlightening. My life had been changed. I was delivered from all fear and insecurity and was taken to the place where I died and Christ took my place. As Paul taught the Galatians: *"It is no longer I who live, but Christ lives in me."* I was relieved to hear that I would not have to pass this way again, and I have enjoyed the benefits of the change God has wrought in my life. My journey to the High Places had really become one of faith.

During this time of growth, I came to realize it is not my ability that will take me higher, but only His ability and grace working in me. At one of the lowest points in my life — physically, spiritually, emotionally and financially — I felt higher than I had ever been before!

God must deal with our pride, fears, insecurities and weaknesses as we climb higher. His ultimate goal is for us to be transformed into His own image. When we die to ourselves, it seems like (and is, in reality) a very dark time. However, if we are, "... *looking unto Jesus, the author and finisher of our faith, who for the joy that was set before Him endured the cross, despising the shame, and has sat down at the right hand of the throne of God*" (Hebrews 12:2, NKJ), we will know the climb is hard and the price is high, but the reward is well worth it!

In the word repent, *the prefix* re *means "to do again." When we repent, we again become what Jesus wants us to be. We are restored to that place of fellowship. The ending of the word,* pent, *means "higher." When we repent, we can maintain a high level of intimacy with God.*

CHAPTER 10

REPENTANCE: THE WAY TO "PENTHOUSE CHRISTIAN LIVING"

As many as I love, I rebuke and chasten. Therefore be zealous and
REPENT.   Revelation 3:19, NKJ

As we continue to climb to the High Places, we must come to understand the power of repentance. On the mountain of God we all stumble and fall. The mistake that many of us make when this happens is thinking that we must go back to the bottom and start all over again. That is clearly our own idea, for it is not God's way. Through the power of repentance we can pick ourselves up, shake off the sin, and continue to climb. *"Therefore be zealous and REPENT."*

Our challenge seems to lie in the amount of time it takes to acknowledge we have sinned. It is very important to repent before God and move on to take our place on the high road. When we move quickly we don't get stuck in the place where we have sinned. It is part of the maturation process when we learn to look at the place where we were from a heavenly viewpoint, instead of from ground level.

I like the observation point from on high, whether it is from the top of a mountain or from the seat of an airplane. I love looking out of an airplane window and seeing sections of farmland laid out in perfect squares or open land punctuated with flowing streams. From up there it seems that all is well with the world and everything is functioning in the perfection that God created it to work in.

Height gives us a different view, a higher perspective. The world seems more orderly and more unified. From that vantage point we somehow gain a better understanding of "the big picture." There's something about a mountaintop perspective that changes us.

That view from the top is a gift from God. It removes us from the disorder the world is really in and challenges us to look ahead to our eternal future and to free ourselves from the encumbrances of our sin nature. That is what repentance is all about.

While attending a service early last winter, I was intrigued by the perspective on repentance that was being taught from the platform that morning. It opened my eyes to a new level of understanding about repenting to climb higher.

The pastor shared this perspective: In the word *repent*, the prefix *re* means "to do again." When we repent, we again become what Jesus wants us to be. We are restored to a place of fellowship with Him. The ending of the word, *pent*, means "higher," and repentance brings us to a higher level of intimacy with God.

A penthouse is the highest apartment in a building, and usually the best. The Bible says we have been seated with Christ *"in the heavenly places"*:

> *But God, who is rich in mercy, because of His great love with which He loved us, even when we were dead in trespasses, made us alive together with Christ (by grace you have been saved), and raised us up together, and MADE US SIT TOGETHER IN THE HEAVENLY PLACES in Christ Jesus,* Ephesians 2:4-6, NKJ

"Penthouse Christian living," therefore, means living in the High Places through repentance. Many believers, because of past mistakes, are living in the basement when they could be living in the penthouse.

We sometimes think that repentance is just saying "I'm sorry." A declaration of being "sorry" may seem especially convincing if accompanied by tears. Still, words accompanied by tears may not express true repentance. What we are feeling and expressing may be nothing more than remorse. Most people are simply sorry they got caught, and they vow to be more careful the next time. That's bargain-basement remorse, not true repentance before God.

True repentance causes us to say:

"God, I sinned against You and others. I hurt You, and I don't want to do that again. Show me how You view my actions, and teach me how awful that sin was in Your sight. Instruct me so that I will know how to avoid this in the future and turn from that sin and change!"

That is true repentance!

God is not an unjust Creator sitting on a throne just waiting to chastise His children when they are disobedient. He is a loving Father who desires obedient children, not for His benefit, but so that our lives will be blessed, fruitful and full of happiness. Nevertheless, He is a Holy God and demands that His children live holy lives.

Holiness, however, is not a list of rules, regulations and dress codes. Holiness is an issue of the heart. We can live in holiness only when our hearts are wholly given over to God.

John's letter to the churches expresses what I consider to be the principles of penthouse Christian living:

And these things we write to you that your joy may be full. This is the message which we have heard from Him and declare to you, that God is light and in Him is no darkness at all. If we say that we have fellow-ship with him, and walk in darkness, we lie and do not practice the truth. But if we walk in the light as He is in the light, we have fellow-ship with one another, and the blood of Jesus Christ His Son cleanses us from all sin. If we say that we have no sin, we deceive ourselves, and the truth is not in us. If we confess our sins, He is faithful and just to forgive us our sins and to cleanse us from all unrighteousness.

1 John 1:4-9, NKJ

God is not interested in rules and regulations; He is interested in relationship. Many people are deceived into substituting legal-ism for relationship. Legalism results when we live according to men's rules and traditions, believing that this places us in favor with God. Without relationship, such legalism produces death.

In reality, God wants us to walk with Him (in fellowship) in the light. As we do, the Holy Spirit will convict us of our sin and shortcomings and illuminate our darkness with His light (see John 3:20-21). As we confess our sins, the blood of Jesus cleanses and forgives us, and we are changed.

Not only does God show us our sin and then cleanse our sin, He also gives us the grace and power to walk free from the bond-age of that sin.

Paul declared to the Roman believers:

For sin shall not have dominion over you.   Romans 6:14

In the Word of God we see many excellent examples of bar-gain-basement repentance (mere remorse) and true repentance. For instance, in the story of Saul recorded in 1 Samuel, we read that Saul sinned against God through rebellion.

God commanded Saul:

Now go and attack Amalek, and utterly destroy all that they have, and do not spare them. But kill both man and woman, infant and nursing child, ox and sheep, camel and donkey. 1 Samuel 15:3, NKJ

Saul, however, disobeyed God:

But Saul and the people spared Agag and the best of the sheep, the oxen, the fatlings, the lambs, and all that was good, and were unwilling to utterly destroy them. 1 Samuel 15:9, NKJ

The prophet Samuel confronted Saul for his sin:

Then Samuel went to Saul, and Saul said to him, "Blessed are you of the LORD! I have performed the commandment of the LORD." But Samuel said, "What then is this bleating of the sheep in my ears, and the lowing of the oxen which I hear?" And Saul said, "They have brought them from the Amalekites; for the people spared the best of the sheep and the oxen, to sacrifice to the LORD your God; and the rest we have utterly destroyed." 1 Samuel 15:13-15, NKJ

When confronted by the prophet, Saul first blamed his sin on someone else, anyone but himself (see verse 21). He refused to take accountability for his own disobedience. Then, he asked to be restored in the sight of the people (see verse 30). It seems apparent that he was more concerned about his reputation than about rectifying his rebellion against God. The prophet told him:

The LORD has torn the kingdom of Israel from you. Verse 28, NKJ

This is the fruit of bargain-basement repentance. Saul was only sorry that he had been caught, not that he had sinned. This is not true repentance, and his words and actions did nothing to restore his relationship to God. His attitude brought him judgment.

In total contrast to Saul's story, we have the heartrending tale of David's sin (see 2 Samuel 11). David had been exalted from being a mere shepherd boy to ruling in the courts of the palace. David the shepherd boy had become David the king. Although he had experienced many trials and battles on his way to the throne (the High Place), he had come through them all with more trust and love for God.

Then, one restless evening, when everything was going well for him, David's darkest hour came. He was walking on his terrace, enjoying the coolness of the evening, when he spotted Bathsheba bathing on a nearby rooftop. He was tempted by her beauty, sent for her, slept with and impregnated her, had her husband killed, and then took Bathsheba to be his wife.

If sin can be categorized, it seems clear to me that David's sin was far worse than that of Saul. The difference in the two cases, however, becomes clear when we see Nathan the prophet confronting David for his sin. David's repentant spirit is captured in the psalms:

Purge me with hyssop, and I shall be clean;
Wash me, and I shall be whiter than snow.
Make me hear joy and gladness,
That the bones You have broken may rejoice.
Hide Your face from my sins,
And blot out all my iniquities.
Create in me a clean heart, O God.
And renew a steadfast spirit within me.
Do not cast me away from Your presence,
And do not take Your Holy Spirit from me.
Restore to me the joy of Your salvation,
And uphold me by Your generous Spirit.

Psalm 51:7-12, NKJ

This was true repentance, and the result of it was David's restoration.

Now, why would God restore one king and not the other? It clearly was not because David's sin was less severe. It was not. It was because of the difference in the attitude of the two men toward their relationship with God. Both men sinned in the eyes of the Lord, and sin is sin. In one sense of the word, we could say that one sin is not greater than another. David, however, was forgiven because he sought God's heart on the matter, and Saul was not because he sought to justify himself.

David did not get off scot-free. The price of his sin was devastating. His entire family suffered because of it, and blood never left his household. When David passed from this life, however, he died with the reputation of being *"a man after God's own heart,"* for his heart belonged wholly to God.

The Bible states:

He maketh my feet like hinds' feet and setteth me upon my high places.
Psalm 18:33

I am told that these animals dwell in high mountains and are extremely sure-footed. Even when they fall, somehow they land on their feet without injury. David sang:

When I said, My foot slippeth; thy mercy, O LORD, held me up.
Psalm 94:18

Through God's mercy, our feet can be kept from slipping. Our feet can be made *"like hinds' feet."* Through repentance and faith in God's mercy, we can enjoy "penthouse Christian living."

The test of our level of achievement in God's Kingdom is not what we have done in His name, but our intimate, personal relationship with Him!

CHAPTER 11

DWELLING IN THE SECRET PLACE OF
THE MOST HIGH

He who dwells in the secret place of the Most High
Shall abide under the shadow of the Almighty.

Psalm 91:1-2, NKJ

As we study the Word of God, we realize that His ultimate desire for us is to have intimate fellowship with Him. Adam and Eve were created for fellowship. When they fell because of sin, it was such a tragic moment that we have come to call it "The Great Fall."

To fall from a place indicates that you must have achieved a certain level of height. Adam and Eve had experienced the ultimate high of knowing God, not only as Creator, but also as Friend. It was from that place of divine intimacy with God that they fell when they chose to disobey Him.

After Adam and Eve had sinned and fallen, God went looking for them. *"Where are you?"* He called (Genesis 3:9). The sad truth is that Adam and Eve were hiding from their Creator. They knew they had sinned, so they were afraid of God and hid from Him. They were suddenly conscious of their nakedness and wanted to hide it. Their intimacy with the Almighty had been shattered, and their first instinct was to stay in the shadows and hide from the presence of God.

This feeling of shame that Adam and Eve experienced is universal. We all feel uncovered when we have sinned, and when this happens we tend to hide and to run from God just as they did. The reality is that we need to do the opposite. Don't run FROM God, run TO Him.

To purge the sin of Adam, God instituted the blood covenant and clothed Adam and Eve in the skins of the animals that were thus sacrificed (see Genesis 3:21). This was a type, or shadow, of the price Jesus would one day pay so that our fellowship (intimacy) with God could be restored. Just as He redeemed Adam, His desire is to redeem every one of us.

There are so many examples in the Bible that show us how very much God desires intimacy and relationship with His creation that no room is left for doubt. He is actively pursuing us and drawing us unto Himself.

The Word of God speaks of Enoch, who *"walked with God and ... was not"* (Genesis 5:24). Enoch just disappeared from the Earth one day. God enjoyed his fellowship so much that one day He said to His servant, "I so enjoy your company that I want you to come on up and stay with Me continually." Enoch was never seen again by his family or friends. He had gone to be with God.

Several portions of scripture call Abraham *"the friend of God"* (see James 2:23). Why is that? It is because Abraham knew the importance of intimacy with the Creator.

Of Moses, God said, "To my prophets I speak in dreams and similitudes, but to My servant Moses I speak *'face to face, as a friend speaks to his friend'* " (Exodus 33:11). On one occasion, Moses had said to God, *"If Your presence does not go with me, I don't want to go"* (Exodus 33:15).

The Apostle Paul, in New Testament times, recognized the importance of intimacy with God and declared, *"I give up everything just to know Him"* (Philippians 3:8-10).

All of these men were hungry, but not for power, miracles or the anointing (although these aspects of God's character are also important). They were hungry for fellowship and intimacy with the Most High God.

I have often thanked God for the opportunities I have had to know many of the great men and women of God of this age. It has been a privilege and an honor to call them friends. It has been an incredible experience to learn from them. Although I have been blessed by these natural relationships, the greatest blessing is to realize that God, the Most High, has called us to be His friends. He said:

> *No longer do I call you servants, for a servant does not know what his master is doing; but I have called you friends, for all things that I heard from My Father I have made known to you.*   John 15:15, NKJ

The most exciting and fulfilling times I have ever experienced have been in deep, intimate personal fellowship with the Most High God. When I first got saved, because of our cramped living conditions, I would go to the parking lot of a local Wal-Mart, lock myself in the car, and sing to the Lord. It was wonderful!

The Word of God declares:

> *Come before His presence with singing.*   Psalm 100:2

When you begin to worship the Lord, you will learn to walk with Him. And as you walk with Him, you will be enabled to work for Him.

Worship is the way into fellowship with God. Just as incense was burnt before the veil of the Holy of Holies, our worship is as incense that rises up before God and opens our pathway into fellowship with Him.

Jesus said:

> *Many will say to Me in that day, "Lord, Lord, have we not prophesied in Your name, cast out demons in Your name, and done many wonders in Your name?" And then I will declare to them, "I never knew you; depart from Me."*   Matthew 7:22-23, NKJ

What terrible words: DEPART FROM ME! Jesus will be forced to say *"I never knew you"* to those who fail to maintain an intimate relationship with Him. Once we are saved, the test of our level of achievement in God's Kingdom is not what we have done in His name, but the intensity of our intimate, personal relationship with Him. Nothing can take its place.

Recently, while reading in the Old Testament, I came to a story about Elijah, the great prophet. The story goes like this: Elijah was zealous for God and had a God-given, God-ordained desire to replace the evil of his day with the righteousness of the Almighty. We find him, at the height of his ministerial life, on Mount Carmel, calling the people to stop being wishy-washy in their commitment to God. He boldly declared: *"If the LORD is God, follow Him; but if Baal, follow him"* (1 Kings 18:21, NKJ).

We then see Elijah calling fire down from Heaven, mocking Baal's power, and demonstrating that the Lord truly is God. After that he killed all the prophets of Baal and repaired the altar of the Lord that had been broken down. What an awesome demonstration of God's power through His servant!

In the very next chapter we see a most interesting change of events. Jezebel had sent a messenger to Elijah, and the words of the message he bore brought such fear and discouragement to the prophet that he ran for his life to a place called Beersheba. Geographically, Beersheba is the lowest point in Israel. Elijah had gone from Mount Carmel, one of the highest places (physically) in the land, to Beersheba, the lowest point (geographically).

The discouragement Elijah felt became so great that he *"sat under a juniper tree and prayed that he might die"* (1 Kings 19:4). I have spoken to many other servants of God, who, like myself, have had experiences similar to this one of Elijah. We have been blessed by great times of ministry and demonstrations of the power of God, and then the next day or the next night it seems as though God is a million miles away. I believe God allows this to happen to show us that we need to be continually seeking Him to stay in the intimate relationship with Him that sustains us.

God wanted Elijah to make a journey from Mount Carmel to Mount Horeb, so He sent an angel to the prophet to supernaturally strengthen him. The journey was too great for Elijah to make on His own, but he could make it in God's strength. God may ask us to make supernatural journeys, but never without His supernatural help.

Mount Horeb is another name for Mount Sinai. This is the mountain where Moses had intimate contact with the glory of God, so much so that his face shone with God's glory (see Exodus 34:29). This was the spot where God wanted to deal with Elijah. He would take him from Mount Carmel, the place of power and victory, to Mount Horeb, the place of intimacy. The only condition was that he had to go through Beersheba, the lowest place, to get there.

When Elijah got to Mount Horeb, a strong wind blew, an earthquake shook the ground, and a fire raged, but God was not in these powerful demonstrations. He chose to come to Elijah in a still, small voice. This was the place of intimacy that God was revealing to Elijah, the still, small voice that abides in all of us and gives us the ability to know God's will for our lives. This is the work of His precious Holy Spirit.

Coming into this place of intimacy with God changed the whole direction of Elijah's life, just like it will yours. When we see him next, he has a changed heart. He is no longer concerned for himself or his ministry. God has placed within him the Father's heart and a desire to go and anoint Elisha to take his place. He did so, in obedience to God's command (see 1 Kings 19).

God is raising up men and women who have traveled from Mount Carmel to Mount Horeb. They know and have experienced the power and demonstration of God, but they have also traveled through Beersheba and refused to stop there. They have continued on and come to Mount Horeb, the place where the still, small voice of God is heard, and their hearts have been changed forever.

It is in this place of intimacy with the Most High that we realize our ministries are insignificant without His glory. It is here that our ambitions, jealousies, pride and spirit of competition fade into meaninglessness, and we see only Him. It is in His presence that we are changed.

The people of Israel knew God's acts, and yet they turned away. Moses knew God's ways, and he continually pressed closer to the Father's side (see Psalm 103:7).

I am positive that there is an army of believers that God is calling to live in the High Place of fellowship with Him. This will be the generation that brings the Lord's return. These true believers make up the Elijah company that will precede Christ's coming, turning the hearts of the fathers to the sons and of the sons to the fathers. Because of their intimacy with the Lord, these people will have only His kingdom and His agenda in their hearts.

In the very early days of my Christian walk I went through an identity crisis. I felt as though I was in a battle for my very soul. I had thoughts that I now know were assignments against my mind from the pit of Hell. Doubts plagued me about the reality of

God and whether or not I was really called into the ministry. I was tortured by questions for which I had no answers. One night I tossed and turned in my bed, my mind filled with anxiety and fear that I was making the wrong choices and that God had never spoken to me. I got up, went and sat down on the couch and said, "God, if You are real, I need to know it. If You are really who You say You are, then You can speak to me — right here and right now. I don't need to hear from a man. I have read Your Word, and I know that You speak through it, but right here, right now, I need to hear Your voice."

God knows when we are serious. He knows when we are really seeking Him, and He knows what is in our hearts, even more than we do. That night, as I poured my heart out to Someone I wasn't even sure existed, I literally emptied myself out before Him. I didn't want to question our relationship any longer. I not only wanted it settled once and for all, I knew that it had to be settled in my heart before I could go a step further.

As I sat there waiting — for what, I wasn't sure — God spoke to me like a mighty rushing river. His voice did not come from the outside in, but from the inside out. He said these words:

Yea, though you walk through the valley of the shadow of death, fear no evil, for I am with you. My rod and My staff will comfort you.

From that moment on I knew that God was with me. My personal, intimate relationship with Him is what has sustained, enriched and trained me and is enabling me to continue my climb to the High Places. In the years that followed, this promise sustained and prepared me for the battles ahead. There have been many, but we have His promise:

I will never leave you nor forsake you.   Hebrews 13:5, NKJ

We have Jesus as our intimate Friend. It is through Him and Him alone that our work for His Kingdom is accomplished. He not only calls us, He also equips us through our relationship with Him. Making the journey in God's Kingdom is about relationship. Jesus said:

> *Seek ye first the kingdom of God, and His righteousness: and all these things shall be added unto you.* Matthew 6:33

Making the journey is about seeking Him *"first."*

The following principles spoke volumes to me as I contemplated my spiritual journey.

1. *Once you start, never look back.*
2. *Never look beside you to see how well someone else is doing.*
3. *Never take your eyes off the finish line until you have crossed it.*

CHAPTER 12

FINISHING WELL:
THE HIGHEST PLACE

I have fought the good fight, I have finished the race, I have kept the faith.　　　　　　　　　　　　　　　　　　　　　2 Timothy 4:7

Here I am on another airplane, headed to another adventure, pursuing the High Call of God. The safety instructions have been given, the seat belt is tightened, and the trays and seat backs have been secured. It is all too familiar. The plane leaves ground level, and we are headed for our thirty-five-thousand-feet cruising altitude, as we make our way to the next destination.

I am thinking ahead to the day when I will make my last journey, not to a preaching engagement or on a missions trip, but when at last I embark for my final destination, when my last assignment on Earth is completed and eternity is my last landing. There I will stand before the Most High God.

My finite mind can barely comprehend it, but the Scriptures tell us that one day we will each stand before the Most High and be judged according to our work here on Earth. Part of me gets excited about that day, but part of me still questions: Will I be found faithful? Will I have fulfilled my calling? Will I have finished my course with joy? Will my destiny be secured? These are questions I believe we should all ask ourselves.

The Bible shows that on that day some who were *"first"* will be *"last,"* and some who were *"last"* will be *"first"* (Matthew 20:16). The Apostle Paul put it this way:

> *I have fought the good fight, I have finished the race, I have kept the faith. Finally, there is laid up for me the crown of righteousness, which the Lord, the righteous Judge, will give to me on that Day, and not to me only but also to all who have loved His appearing.*
>
> 2 Timothy 4:7-8, NKJ

There IS a reward for those who finish the race. Many start strongly but end weakly. Many run for some distance but are not able to endure to the end. The fight is hard, and the road is rocky and narrow. The journey is long, but there IS a prize to those who finish:

> *Do you not know that those who run in a race all run, but one receives the prize? Run in such a way that you may obtain it. And everyone who competes for the prize is temperate in all things. Now they do it to obtain a perishable crown, but we for an imperishable crown. Therefore I run thus: not with uncertainty. Thus I fight: not as one who beats the air. But I discipline my body and bring it into subjection, lest, when I have preached to others, I myself should become disqualified.*
>
> 1 Corinthians 9:24-27, NKJ

Paul kept his body *"under subjection."* He did not allow His earthly desires or emotions to dictate his destiny. He was determined to finish the race, and he ran expecting to win. He was fully expecting to obtain the prize.

Pastor Benny Hinn, who, as I have shown, has had a huge impact on my life, recently shared a story with me about his childhood days when he ran races in school. He said that his coach gave very specific instructions for the race:

1. Once you start, never look back.
2. Never look beside you to see how well someone else is doing.
3. Never take your eyes off the finish line until you have crossed it.

These words spoke volumes to me as I contemplated my spiritual journey. Jesus said:

No man, having put his hand to the plow, and looking back, is fit for the kingdom of God.   Luke 9:62

We should never look back but should press on toward the future. We should never be concerned about how fast or slow others are running their race, and we should never be caught examining the spiritual growth or lack thereof of others. We must stay focused on our own journey, for we each run on a different path. We must get our eyes fixed on our own goal. As the writer of the book of Hebrews declared:

Let us run with endurance the race that is set before us, looking unto Jesus [our finish line], the author and finisher of our faith.
                                                   Hebrews 12:1-2, NKJ

It is by faith that we finish the race. Many men and women have set examples of faith for us to follow, and it is clear from their records that it was only through trusting God that they were able to run the race and finish well. Such men and women are familiar to those of us who love the Bible:

By faith Abraham, when he was tried, offered up Isaac ... accounting [concluding] that God was able to raise him up, even from the dead.
Hebrews 11:17-19

By faith Moses, when he became of age, refused to be called the son of the Pharaoh's daughter ... for he looked to the reward.
Hebrews 11:24-26, NKJ

By faith the harlot Rahab did not perish ... when she had received the spies with peace.
Hebrews 11:31, NKJ

There were many others who accomplished great things for God's Kingdom — *"by faith."* They are all witnesses to us, as modern-day believers, so that we can also endure and finish well. The greatest of all examples to us, of course, was Jesus Christ Himself, and He is *"the author and finisher of our faith."* Like many of the saints that came before and after Him, He endured many hardships. His example clearly defines the reality that faith does not keep us FROM trials, tragedies or painful experiences, but keeps us THROUGH them.

Faith in the work of the cross enables us to victoriously run the race, whatever obstacles may come our way. By setting our sights on Jesus and trusting His sacrifice, we are acknowledging that the work is truly finished.

Acts 20:24 confirms what our attitude should be:

But none of these things move me, neither count I my life dear unto myself, so that I might finish my course with joy, and the ministry, which I have received of the Lord Jesus, to testify the gospel of the grace of God.
Acts 20:24

When we have this perspective, each trial becomes another

opportunity to see God's hand bringing us into the High Place of becoming more Christ-like.

Faith is not a lifeboat, but it is safe passage through the trial.

Many have successfully run the race of faith, and we can look to their examples and be encouraged, but, again, the greatest of them was Jesus:

> *Who for the joy that was set before Him endured the cross, despising the shame, and has sat down at the right hand of the throne of God.*
>
> Hebrews 12:2, NKJ

Jesus *"endured the cross,"* not only to reconcile us back into right relationship with our heavenly Father, but also to make us overcomers in this present life. We are to be overcomers HERE and NOW.

In the Revelation given to John on the Isle of Patmos, Jesus described our benefits as overcoming Christians:

> *To him that overcometh will I give to eat of the tree of life, which is in the midst of the paradise of God* [God's presence].   Revelation 2:7

> *Be thou faithful unto death, and I will give thee a crown of life… He that overcometh shall not be hurt of the second death* [we will not taste death].   Verses 10-11

> *To him that overcometh will I give to eat of the hidden manna, and will give him a white stone, and in the stone a new name written, which no man knoweth saving he that receiveth it.* [God will give you new revelation when you feed on Jesus, the Bread of Life; as you exchange your old nature for Christ's character, God will write His name upon your new nature.]   Verse 3

He that overcometh, and keepth my works unto the end, to him will I give power over the nations:
And I will give him the morning star.   Revelation 2:26 and 28

As overcomers, you will reign with Jesus, share His victory over evil, and receive the ultimate reward of Jesus Himself, the Bright Morning Star!

In my personal walk with Jesus, I have failed miserably many times, but I have learned that by faith I can continue to press on and run the race, letting Him turn my failures into faithfulness, my fears into faith and my tragedies into triumphs. I don't profess to have attained perfection, for there truly is none perfect except Christ, yet I have made the choice to be an overcomer by faith and allow Him to do the rest.

What an ultimate high it will be to stand before the Most High God, before billions of saints of God and tens of thousands of angels of Heaven, and hear His words: *"Well done, My good and faithful servant. Enter into the Kingdom which has been prepared for you from the foundations of the world!"* In that moment we will know, as never before, that there is *No High Like THE MOST HIGH!*

Paul wrote to the churches:

Not as though I had already attained, either were already perfect: but I follow after, if that I may apprehend that for which also I am apprehended of Christ Jesus. Brethren, I count not myself to have apprehended: but this one thing I do, forgetting those things which are behind, and reaching forth unto those things which are before, I press toward the mark for the prize of THE HIGH CALLING OF GOD in Christ Jesus.   Philippians 3:12-14

If you have yet to embark upon your journey to the High Places of God, you can begin right now. The Bible states very clearly that God's promise is for *"whosoever"*:

> *And it shall come to pass, that whosoever shall call on the name of the Lord shall be saved.*   Acts 2:21

Becoming one of God's children is as simple as confessing with your mouth that you believe in your heart that Jesus is the Christ, the Son of God. Once you do that, get ready for the greatest high you have ever known before. And let Him take you higher every single day, until you reach the ultimate high of being in His presence eternally.

If you are already on the mountain making your climb, continue looking to Jesus, the Author and Finisher of your faith. By the grace of God, I will meet you at the top. There we will stand together in the presence of the Most High God and rejoice that He has made our climb to the heights possible, for truly there is *No High Like THE MOST HIGH*!

Not as though I had already attained, either were already perfect: but I follow after, if that I may apprehend that for which also I am apprehended of Christ Jesus. Brethren, I count not myself to have apprehended: but this one thing I do, forgetting those things which are behind, and reaching forth unto those things which are before, I press toward the mark for the prize of THE HIGH CALLING OF GOD in Christ Jesus.   Philippians 3:12-14